THE
TURKISH
AMBASSADOR

EMIR KIVIRCIK

The translater: Stuart Kline
The proof reader: Betsy Göksel
The commercial editor: Ellen Reisman

ISBN: 1453677305
ISBN-13: 9781453677308
Library of Congress Control Number: 2010911524

I am indebted to his Excellency Abdullah Gül, President of the Turkish Republic, who was instrumental in helping me gain access to the Turkish Ministry of Foreign Affairs archives.

I am also indebted to his Excellency Shimon Peres, President of Israel, for his encouragement written to me on April 2, 2008. In that letter he wrote, "I hope you will be heard by many."

AUTHOR'S NOTE

This biographical novel is based on archival material most of which has been reproduced in a number of papers published in highly refereed academic journals and in three highly documented and widely reviewed history books. However, in writing this book I have used the texture and devices of many classic novels which told a true story. Yet, I have attempted to avoid fiction as fiction will debase the record and the readers' ability to distinguish between reality and the myth. While all of the characters in this book are real, I have taken dramatic liberties and literary license in cases where the actual dialog has not been made part of recorded history. For source materials the reader may wish to refer to Professor Stanford Shaw's 1993 book *Turkey and the Holocaust* and/or Professor Arnold Reisman's *SHOAH: Turkey, the US, and the UK* published in 2009 or better yet *An Ambassador and A Mensch: The story of a Turkish Diplomat in Vichy France* published in 2010.

This book is in memory of an illustrious General, a Parliamentarian, a Minister and an Ambassador who saved many lives during the Holocaust, Behic Erkin - my maternal Grandfather.

ACKNOWLEDGEMENTS

* * *

I wish to thank all those who selflessly committed their time and efforts to the production of this book. Among them are historian Cemal Kutay, historian Prof. Stanford Shaw, historian Harry Ojalvo, historian Prof. Temucin Ertan, Ambassador Osman Korutürk, Ambassador Necdet Kent, Ambassador Namık Kemal Yolga, Ambassador Oğuz Gökmen, and Ambassador Tansuğ Bleda.

I would like to thank Mehmet Çelebi for his wholehearted support.

I also want to thank my wife, my son, my daughter, and my brother, all of whom gave me their full support in this task which required them to be immensely patient with me.

I am especially grateful to Yechiel Bar-Chaim for his great support and making sacrifices from his time, which is immensely precious.

I would like to thank Paul Polansky for his perceptive criticism and always pertinent suggestions.

Last but not least, I am infinitely grateful to my dear mother, Neyran Erkin, the guiding light in helping me write this book.

Dear Dr. Alfred Bader, without you my dream
would have never become a reality. Words
fail me in showing my gratitude.

To the memory of those who weren't saved

and

To the memory of a heroic mother who made a decision
for her seven month old baby
that no one should ever have to face.

CONTENTS

⊠⊠

MRS. BLUM'S VISIT

On September 21, 1942, Sedat Zeki, Undersecretary at the Turkish Embassy in Vichy, France, informed Behiç Erkin, the Ambassador, that a very intriguing visitor wanted to see him.

Mrs. Renée Blum, daughter -in-law of Leon Blum, the former French Prime Minister was urgently seeking a meeting with the Ambassador.

Standing by the window, his hands clasped behind him, the Ambassador was fidgeting with his prayer beads. The decision to meet with Mrs. Blum would have been difficult for most people since Leon Blum was locked in jail.

Blum's trial had been stopped by the Germans the previous April because the eloquent, 70 year-old politician had exposed the treason charges against him for what they were -a ridiculous farce. Erkin knew it would be uncomfortable for his country to get involved with the internationally known Jewish socialist but without a moment of hesitation he ordered, "Well, just don't stand there, Zeki; show the woman in."

Looking at Zeki as the man left the room he mused, "A fifty year old undersecretary never becomes an ambassador if he fears making decisions".

Moments later Mrs. Blum, an attractive woman in her late 30s, entered the office. Dressed in black as if she were attending a funeral she thanked the Ambassador for meeting with her without an appointment. Despite her attempt to keep her composure, she was quite distressed and obviously needed to discuss something important.

Assuming she had come to ask for help for her father-in-law whose situation was quite desperate in the hands of the Vichy French government, Erkin allowed her a few moments to gather her thoughts and catch her breath. He had met Leon Blum only once, shortly after his arrival in Paris in September 1939 when he was installed as the new Turkish ambassador.

"What I'm about to tell you may seem a bit strange, but my father-in-law said that you were the only person who could help because of your positive relationship with the Germans and because you respect and support your Jewish citizens."

"I'm afraid, Madame, that what your father-in-law believes isn't exactly correct. As far as the current French government or the Germans in Vichy are concerned, we don't have 'relationships' nor are we here to establish friendships; we're here to carry out the responsibilities assigned to us. Perhaps the fact that my embassy operates smoothly gave the wrong impression.

As far as our Jewish citizens are concerned, you must realize that I'm from a country which has never been enslaved. Consequently I have trouble understanding how the leaders of France could meekly allow their country to be enslaved by an enemy and do that enemy's bidding without much of a fight. In fact, these French officials often out-German the Germans in their treatment of French Jewish citizens. At this moment, we at the Turkish Embassy are protecting the rights of our citizens who live here whether they are Muslim, Christian, or Jewish."

Mrs. Blum, who had been listening with rapt attention, looked down at her hands, collected her thoughts, and took a deep breath.

"The reason why I am here, Mr. Ambassador, has nothing to do with my father in law's situation; that is, I'm here because of my husband. What is happening to my husband is causing my father-in-law even more stress than he already has."

Trying to jog his memory for the bits and pieces he had heard about the Blum family, Erkin recalled that Leon Blum's only son was a prisoner of war.

"My husband and the men captured with him are being tortured and held in isolation in a POW camp in Germany. My father-in-law fears that h's son is being treated this way simply because his name is Blum....and that his fellow officers are suffering because they are with him."

Now Erkin remembered. The camp she was talking about, Camp Oflag Xc, was one of the many camps built to house officers only. This particular camp was in Lubeck and held other French VIP notables such as historian Fernand Braudel (1902-1985) and brothers Elie (1917-2007) and Alain (1910-1982)de Rothschild, sons of Robert de Rotchschild (1880-1946).

"My father in law suggested that I come here, explain the situation, and ask for your help."

Answering slowly, carefully, and considering each word Erkin replied, "Unfortunately, I'm not convinced my involvement would be beneficial nor have the political influence that you obviously desire. But dry your eyes and allow me to finish."

Leaning forward to emphasize his words and looking directly into Madame Blum's eyes, Erkin explained his precarious position and his idea.

"During the process of protecting the rights of thousands of our citizens, it is imperative that we consider every detail with extreme caution so we don't ruin the delicate balance in our sensitive relations with the French and German authorities. We don't have the luxury of making a wrong move in an environment where just one misstep can cost the lives of many people. At this stage, considering our involvement in other matters, it would be inappropriate for the ambassador of a neutral country to help the POW son of the former French Prime Minister who is imprisoned on charges of treason. Having said that, there is something I can suggest. Visit your father-in-law as soon as possible and ask him to write a letter explaining the matter and address it to the Esteemed President of Turkey, İsmet İnönü. Bring that letter to me. I'll add a cover letter and make sure it reaches President İnönü. It might be better to try and solve this from Turkey, not here."

"And what if your president refuses?"

"Madame Blum, I didn't say the Turkish Minister of Foreign Affairs or the Turkish Prime Minister. I said the President himself. I know him personally which is why I'll be writing the cover letter."

After Mrs. Blum left, looking a bit more hopeful than when she arrived, Undersecretary Zeki commented about the sad state of affairs in which the great Prime Minister of France was...

"The former Prime Minister of France," Erkin reminded him.

"It doesn't matter; he was this country's Prime Minister. Now he's asking the Turkish Embassy to help his son who is being tortured in a Nazi prisoner of war camp. Isn't this situation analogous to the time when King François the First was imprisoned by the Spanish and had to ask Sultan Süleyman the Magnificent to intercede?"

"Well, history does repeat itself."

The next day, having visited her father- in- law in his jail cell in Bourassol where he had been languishing for two years, Mrs. Blum returned to the Turkish Embassy with a letter which had been scribbled in pencil and signed by the former Prime Minister of France, Leon Blum.

This one page note, addressed to Turkish President İsmet İnönü, requested assistance in saving his son and his son's compatriots who were held in Camp Oflag Xc .

As promised, Erkin transmitted that letter to Ankara on the same day and not long thereafter a letter was received from the Turkish President. President İnönü stated that he had met with Von Papen, the German Ambassador whereupon Leon Blum's son and his cohorts were released from isolation and were being treated as ordinary prisoners of war. Blum senior was apprised of the developments via French General Watteau.

Shortly before Leon Blum was transferred to Buchenwald concentration camp in Germany in February of 1943, his daughter-in-law returned to the Turkish Embassy to personally thank Behiç Erkin and give him a pencil written letter[1] from the former French Prime Minister. At first glance it appeared that Blum was expressing his gratitude to President İnönü for saving the life of his son, but he knew that the mastermind behind the operation was Behiç Erkin. Therefore, the letter was addressed to the Ambassador and sent to the Turkish Embassy.

Bourassol, 22 February
Mr. Ambassador,

I ask you to accept my most cordial thanks for the care you took in seeing to it that I learned the good news from President İnönü. But I ask you as well — permit me to say to you, I beg of you especially — to transmit to President İsmet İnönü the expression of my profound gratitude. I owe him the most comfort and relief that can be offered me in the present conditions of my personal life. What adds further to my satisfaction is that his friendly intervention did not only benefit my son, but also all his fellow camp prisoners with whom he will from now on share his fate.

Please accept what I ask of you, Mr. Ambassador ; I give the assurance of my respectful and warm appreciation.

---

1   see Appendix 1 for orignal letter written in French

THE MEMOIRS

* * *

When I was 16 years old my mother, Neyran Erkin, sat me down and began to relate stories about my grandfather's brother, Behiç. I already knew about his role at Gallipoli in the First World War, his part in the Turkish War of Liberation, and all the medals he had won. Like many teenage boys only interested in sports, I found these stories rather dull and boring and wanting to be excused, made no secret of that fact. Upset and disappointed, Mom never spoke to me about Behic Erkin again.

Sixteen years later as a young businessman with weighty issues on my mind I arranged to meet a friend for lunch; but when I arrived he was still in a meeting which would continue for another hour. This friend worked for Profilo, a large company owned by Jak Kamhi, a prominent Jewish businessman. Standing there trying to decide how to kill an hour, I noticed on the directory that there was a museum in the basement so I went downstairs. It was possible that I could learn something.

The elevator doors opened and I was greeted by an elderly man who was surprised that I knew about this museum. Explaining that my friend worked in the building and I was not there by accident, he offered to show me around. He turned the lights on and introduced himself as Harry Ojalvo, the museum director.

Mr. Ojalvo began our tour by explaining that this Museum of the Quincentennial Foundation founded by Jak Kamhi, was all about Turkish Jews. Well, I was killing time and not really all that keen on the subject until I noticed a sign with the date 1492. Curious, I inquired about its significance and Harry told me about the **Alhambra Decree** (also known as the **Edict of Expulsion**), which ordered the expulsion of all Jews from the Kingdom of Spain, including its territories and possessions, by July 31, 1492. That decree had been issued on March 31 of that year by the joint Catholic Monarchs of Spain, Isabella the First and Ferdinand the Second. The Jews who chose to remain either converted to Christianity or were executed. Harry explained that many who did leave were murdered by pirates "until the Ottoman Sultan Beyazid the Second sent a fleet of ships and welcomed the Spanish Jews to the Ottoman Empire. They settled in Thessaloniki, Sarajevo, İstanbul, and in parts of Anatolia."

Perhaps it was because I'm not Jewish that I never heard the story before and found it fascinating. As we walked around the museum

Harry pointed out various pictures and items of interest.

He showed me some pictures of Jewish scientists and asked if I knew the story of these men and how the founder of our Turkish Republic, Mustafa Kemal Atatürk, had helped them to leave Nazi Germany in the 1930s.

Like many graduates of the University of Istanbul where those Jewish scientists had worked as teachers and re-searchers, I knew that they had been instrumental in the modernization of our education system but never thought of them as refugees.   When we arrived at the part of the museum that was about World War II, the memorabilia of that era contained records of the Turkish diplomats who had rescued thousands of Jews from France and a few from Rhodes during the Holocaust.

Harry pointed out a list of those heroes which was titled: "Honor List of the Turkish Diplomats Who Saved Jews during the Dark Period of World War II."

I looked… I was shocked! I couldn't catch my breath and I looked again, closer!

I know I must have frightened Mr. Ojalvo because he looked concerned that something was wrong with me, especially when I shouted, "That first name on the list! It's Behiç Erkin!

"Well, yes! He headed the Turkish diplomats in France."

I became more and more excited. "My God, I didn't know that!"

"What's the matter? Are you all right?"

"My mother.....Her name is Neyran Erkin."

Harry was a bit shocked by my outbursts and we just stared at each other for a while, speechless.

Like pieces of a puzzle that suddenly come together, I realized the importance of what Mom had been trying to tell me years ago. Sheepishly I admitted to Harry that she made so many attempts to share stories about him but because I found them boring, she never went beyond the 1920s.

"You have to be kidding me!" Those are the words Harry used, but it sounded more like, "You jerk!" Reacting to my chagrin, Harry said it would be an honor for him to tell me about Behiç Erkin. For the next hour, I learned what had happened in France during WWII, how thousands of Jews were rescued by Turkish diplomats, and what Turkish Ambassador Behiç Erkin's role had been. I was embarrassed of my ignorance of my family's history and ashamed of my behavior towards my mother years ago, blowing off the opportunity to learn because of more interesting things to do. Calling my mother from the museum, I introduced her to Harry and the two of them spent hours on the phone.

I never went to lunch with my friend that day. Instead, I went straight home from the museum and asked Mom to tell me the entire story of Behiç Erkin, my Grandpa Behic! Because he regarded my mom whom he adopted as his daughter and helped raise her and because he had no grandchildren, he was our grandfather. I know Mom was pleased by my request and she was willing to oblige, but she had her conditions. So the cell phone went off and all my plans for the next two days went out the window. My mother spoke and I listened.

Behiç Erkin came from a long line of famous Ottoman army officers. His own grandfather, Omer Fevzi, had been the governor of different Ottoman States and in each he had been the commander of the army. Behiç's father, Cemil, had also served as the district governor of Baghdad and Basra and his uncle who raised him after his parents divorced was a general as well as a governor of Basra.

After graduating from Army Officer's School in 1903, Behic began his upward climb through the military ranks. Along the way he married a general's daughter and in 1915, along with Mustafa Kemal, was instrumental in the victory at Gallipoli during the First World War. As the commander responsible for war logistics, Behiç received many medals from the Ottoman Empire as well as the Iron Cross, 1st Degree, for heroism from their German ally.

Because he had been successful, Erkin was put in charge of logistics during Turkey's War of Liberation (1919-1922), and received the highest Turkish honor known as the "War of Independence Medal "(İstiklal Madalyası). During the early years of the Republic, he became the Minister of Public Works, founder of the Turkish Railways (TCDD), and of the Turkish Pension System (Emekli Sandığı).

After hearing "Grandpa Behiç's" story, I wondered why more people didn't know about him. He had three children but no grandchildren which made my mother his only living relative and, in effect, the last of the Erkin line. Mom said that one of the most interesting periods of Behiç's life was his ambassadorship to Paris between 1939 and 1943. While she may not have known all the details, she did remember that "Grandpa Behiç" had written his memoirs and given them to the Turkish History Association (TTK), and he had given his letters and documents to the

University of Ankara Revolution History Institute Museum. Mom suggested I locate those memoirs and read them carefully. I became a man on a mission, determined to find and read those stories. Never mind that it was 1998, and Behiç had made the donation in 1958. Never mind that those papers had been gathering dust for forty years and could be underneath stacks of other memoirs. Never mind that the trail was as cold as, well, let's just say the trail was very cold!

Undeterred I went to Ankara, to the Turkish History Association. When queried about Behiç Erkin's memoirs, the archivist had no idea what I was talking about and, in a tone implying I was not too bright, asked me if I was sure such a thing had ever been written.

As any child would do in the same situation, I blurted out, "Sure I'm sure! My mother told me so."

That response probably reinforced the archivist's attitude because unimpressed with what I considered an unimpeachable source, I was countered with the notion that just because your mommy says it's so doesn't make it so.... and perhaps she had "misremembered". This schoolyard logic did not sit well with me or my mother who angrily insisted that she was absolutely positive it was there. Back I went to try and convince the archivists to look again but they responded the same way. They didn't have it.

Realizing there was no sense arguing, I went through their card catalog myself and after several hours, came up with the same conclusion. They did not have it and furthermore, I was informed that if it wasn't in the catalog it wasn't in the Turkish History Association (TKK) at all. I can still recall how I felt that day when I left empty-handed.

Behiç had donated his personal items to the University of Ankara so I went to the university's history museum and asked the lady behind the desk if there were any items in the museum that had belonged to Behiç Erkin. Smiling, she looked around and said, "Almost everything you see here was donated by him."

I was ecstatic and it must have been quite obvious. When I introduced myself she immediately contacted her colleagues and asked them to the museum. The six people who arrived were elated to finally meet a member of Behiç Erkin's family; they had been working on the artifacts, which included 39,000 documents, for years. Among those documents was the letter from the Jewish Prime Minister of France, Leon Blum, thanking Behiç for his efforts in his son's predicament.

Now I had my starting point and could begin my research. But that was easier said than done. It wasn't quite that simple because I had to ask for time off from the company in İstanbul where I worked. To make it all work, I took my vacation in installments, the drips and drabs approach, using the time to go to Ankara where I dropped by the TTK just in case the memoirs they thought never existed miraculously appeared.

This project changed my life. The more I researched the more convinced I became that I needed to write a book about Grandpa Behiç and perhaps even make a documentary. I felt as though I was chosen to tell his story and it became my priority. However, there was still an enormous hurdle to overcome. Behic Erkin's memoirs. I believed my mother that Behiç's memoirs were at the TTK and the TTK believed they were not.

* * *

On these research trips to Ankara, I visited various libraries on the off chance that something of interest would turn up. In one of these libraries, I discovered a book published by TTK called *Railroads during the Liberation War*. Knowing Grandpa Behic's involvement with railroads I began to look through it and found exactly what I needed. One of the footnotes in the book chronicled Behiç Erkin's donation of his memoirs to TTK. The book and I went to pay a visit to TTK; I had the proof that my mother was right after all.

With an admitted smugness I located the archivist to inquire if the memoirs could be located. Now that all their records were computerized, I was told that it was easier to determine that there still was no sign of the memoirs. Triumphantly, I slapped the book I had found on the desk and asked that they verify that this book had been published by TTK. Oh, yes, was the reply; it was published by TTK and these publications are always accurate.

"Well then, I would like to ask you a question please. How do you explain this footnote?"

They looked at the book and a long, long silence followed. 1`

In a tone reserved for those particular situations when you know you can't lose, I loudly demanded, "Where are those memoirs?"

The commotion attracted the attention of the library director who assured me nothing ever gets lost in the TTK and the definitive answer would be in the donation ledgers. So off we all went, trotting across the library to the ledgers looking like ducklings following their mother. There it was; the proof for everyone to see. Behiç had donated his memoirs in 1958, but if that was the case, where were they? The library manager had an idea. Telephoning an elderly lady who had retired from the TTK 10 years earlier, she learned where the memoirs were. The archivists were correct. The memoirs were not in the archives! They were in TTK's printing house waiting and waiting and waiting to be published. A few hours later six blue folders were in my hands making that one of the happiest days of my life.

* * *

Behiç Erkin had dictated the memoirs to Georgette, a beautiful French lady who had been his secretary in Paris, in Vichy, and had gone with him to Istanbul until a few years after the war when she returned to her own country.

Naturally, Behiç's memoirs didn't give any detailed information about his physical aspects but he wrote what he considered were important details about his work and life. Yet from these details one can discern the character and personality of the man. The details he did reveal were quite basic facts like, "When my parents got divorced, my aunt and uncle took my mother, Nadire, and me in. My aunt and her husband, who was the governor of Basra at the time, had no children of their own; therefore they loved me as their own son.

My uncle had typhus and I contracted it at a very young age which, unfortunately, led to polio. These afflictions left me with a weak right knee and a slight limp. However, my disability never hindered me in performing my duties whether in the military or in civilian life. My mother passed away on 15 January 1953; she was over 90 years old. I tried to provide her with a decent life. She had the kindest of hearts, and she was the embodiment of the word lady."

* * *

"Grandpa Behiç" was 173 cm (5'8") tall and besides the typhus, polio, and weak leg, he was otherwise very fit. Because his grandfather was Field Marshall Ömer Fevzi, an exception was made and he was accepted into officer's school despite his physical disability and he was the only man in the army who had to use a cane.

Like most officers in those days he had a moustache. However, in 1928 after he became an ambassador, his butler shaved his face and head every day which magnified the intensity of his green eyes. Grandpa was fashionably ahead of his time. He dressed very elegantly always wearing a pearl tiepin and had spats on his shoes.

Behic married Behiye, the daughter of general Reşit from Midilli Island (Lesbos), in 1902 and they had three children: two sons Necit and Vecih, and one daughter, Reşide. Sadly Behiye died in 1934 from an infection following a pedicure. At the time Erkin was the ambassador to Hungary and was very popular with the diplomatic corps, Archduke Leopold, and Admiral Nikolaus von Horthy, Regent of the Kingdom of Hungary. When Behiye died, the flags over all embassies in Hungary flew at half- mast. One of Behic's sons became an architect, the other a businessman, and his daughter often went to Budapest and Paris with him serving as his hostess at his embassy dinners. Sadly, he had no grandchildren.

Like most military men, Grandpa Behiç was regimented, doing everything at a fixed time. Although not particularly a conversationalist, he had a pleasant smile, and was known as a gentleman who always honored the promises he had made. Many people assumed he was a very tough man because he stood up to the Germans in WWII. But although he had a hard stare and a rigid stance, he was sensitive and emotional. He often told my mother that she was the love of his life and his living room was adorned with her school paintings. When he looked at me, I saw that his eyes were always filled with love and affection. His enormous heart was his essential characteristic.

A humble, modest, hard working and disciplined person, he rarely spoke about himself. A Muslim who went to Mosque every Friday, he appeared to believe in God more than the religion itself. His large rented apartment was on the first floor of an elegant old building with high ceilings, designed by an Italian architect. The vast library he had amassed over the years was a testament to his passion for reading. During his retirement, he kept to a routine where he read the newspaper every morning until 10:30 when he exercised his leg and walked until lunch. Although he usually ate alone, all his meals were served in a formal setting. After a short rest, Grandpa would either dictate his memoirs as he sat behind the huge desk he brought from Budapest, or receive guests who had to make appointments well in advance. Unlike so many of his peers he had no car, no chauffeur. He always took a taxi.

His indulgence was cigarettes, but not just any brand. His were custom made which included having his name printed on every single cigarette. But he rarely imbibed. On those occasions when Atatürk and his ministers began to drink, Behiç would simply leave the room.

Other than his childhood illnesses, he was healthy until his death. At that time my mother and her father took turns sitting with Behic and holding his hand until he passed away two days later. Not surprisingly, hundreds of people attended his funeral and his obituary was in every newspaper in Turkey.

* * *

After reading his memoirs, Mom and I agreed that a book about one of "Grandpa Behiç's" least known, most humane, and most rewarding accomplishments, when he was Turkey's ambassador to Paris between 1939 and 1943, ought to be written.

This then is the story of the Turkish Ambassador in Vichy, France.

1939
ANKARA – PARIS

* * *

When Turkish President İsmet İnönü saw the clouds of unrest and recognized imminent war in Europe, he called his friend Behiç Erkin, the recently resigned Minister of Public Works, to his office for consultation. Their trusted friendship went back to the Turkish War of Liberation (1919-1922), in which İnönü had been the Army's Chief of Staff and Behiç had been responsible for transporting Turkish troops and supplies over railways once belonging to the British and the French. Erkin's logistical skills and expertise helped win the war.

With the situation in Europe worsening by the day İnönü believed that two cities were of critical importance to Turkey especially if neutrality was to be maintained. One was Berlin and the other was Paris. Because Turkey needed to be on good terms with Germany and France, Erkin's appointment to one of them as ambassador was extremely important.

At 63 and true to form Erkin replied, "I don't speak German and I don't get along with Germans. When German officers were invited to reform our army during the Ottoman era, I couldn't tolerate taking orders from Germans and they couldn't tolerate the fact that I spoke my mind even in front of the Sultan. However, since my French is quite good I believe that I would be more beneficial in France. "

Shortly after their meeting, Behiç was appointed the Turkish Ambassador to Paris. Behiç's attitudes towards

Germans were so strong that he devoted one section of his memoirs, "My Dealings with the Germans", to expressing his opinions about them and to relating stories about those Germans whom he had encountered. Regarding World War I he explained, "The high ranking German officers at the German Embassy and War Ministry didn't take a liking to me because I didn't execute the duties assigned to my office. As a matter of fact, one day, when I met General Enver by chance in the foyer, his German military attaché exclaimed, 'Behiç, your performance has reached the point that it might ruin the German–Turkish alliance.' And I countered with, "If I've got such great power and authority, then that's something to be proud of, isn't it?"

This attitude of his towards the Germans was corroborated by General Hans Kannengiesser in his book, *The Campaign in Gallipoli*. Kannengiesser had his doubts as to whether Behiç really liked Germans. "I can't tell whether Behiç, below the surface, is an actual friend of Germany. General Enver wanted to reorganize the Turkish army according to German methods. However, I don't think Behiç fully supported or even appreciated this idea."

* * *

Behiç arrived in Paris on Sunday morning, August 13, 1939 and was received by the outgoing Turkish Ambassador, General Kazım Orbay, his ambassadorial staff, and Monsieur Dulignier of the French Foreign Affairs Protocol Office. At a meeting with French Foreign Minister Georges Bonnet, he was informed that he would have to wait to present his credentials to the President until mid-September when the President returned from his vacation. Vacation? With war on France's doorstep, how could a president go on a vacation? This made no sense and Behiç wondered about the nonchalant attitude. He didn't have to wonder for very long. Recognizing the critical state of the political climate, President Albert Lebrun returned to Paris on August 29. That same day, the French Protocol Office informed the Turkish Ambassador that an audience with President Lebrun had been scheduled for the following day. At 11:30 the next morning Behiç and his attendants went to the Elysée Palace, presented their credentials, and joined the other 61 foreign missions in France. He was announced as the new Turkish Ambassador to Paris on August 31, 1939.

When Behic initially arrived in Paris, he had conducted a brief inspection of his embassy noting that compared to other Turkish Embassies in Europe, his staff was the smallest. He wired the Turkish Ministry of Foreign Affairs and had Beşir Balcıoğlu and Melih Esenbel appointed to Paris. Leon Mandil, a Jewish clerk, was fluent in French and wrote all of the embassy's French correspondence. The other ambassadorial staff members were Undersecretary Sedat Zeki Örs, Chief Clerk Fatin Rüştü Zorlu, 3rd clerks Melih Esenbel and Beşir Balcıoğlu, and local Clerks Sadi Eldem and Reşat Temizer. All of these men were graduates of the prestigious Lyceé de Galatasaray in Istanbul.

One day after Behic was formally accepted as the Turkish Ambassador to France, Germany invaded Poland. Two days later England and France declared war on Germany. Diplomatically speaking, all hell had broken loose!

The night of September 4, was the beginning of a weary and sleepless month for the citizens of Paris. As a precaution, sirens shrieked nearly every evening waking the populace, forcing them to leave their beds and seek shelter, thus imposing an atmosphere of anxiety and dread on an already weary and sleep deprived people. Frequent at first, the sirens gradually diminished though blackouts were a nightly occurrence.   Known as the *Phony War*, this period lasted from the day

France declared war on the Germany, September 3, until May 10, 1940, the day German troops entered France.

Behiç noted in memoirs that "Regardless of being at war, the most important weapon is always intelligence. If one is able to learn what the other side is going to do, or even if one has just some information, one is able to plan the next step to be taken, thereby reducing one's risks."

Wasting no time, Behiç met with as many ambassadors as possible and established relations within French government circles. One of his most important contacts was M. Sarraut the French Interior Minister, whom Behiç had met years earlier when Sarraut was the French Ambassador to Turkey. As ambassador it was necessary for Behic to make contacts socially as well as politically. Discussions at parties and dinners often revealed vital information. At one party hosted by Egyptian Ambassador Fahri Pasha, Behic met Madame Georgina Jean Brunhes and Madame Abrami. Madame Brunhes was a wealthy widow who routinely held soirees inviting ministers, diplomats, academicians, generals, and aristocrats. Madame Abrami, the wife of a well-known French doctor, enjoyed entertaining VIPs to learn all the latest political gossip. Thanks to these two women, Behiç had the opportunity to meet several people who were politically influential such as Daladier the former Prime Minister; Paul Reynaud; the current Prime Minister, as well as the General Secretary of Foreign Affairs, Alexi Leger; the French Parliament Speaker, Herriot; General Mougin; the former Ambassador to Berlin, Monsieur Coulondre; the Foreign Minister, Georges Bonnet; and Champetier de Ribes, soon to be the Foreign Minister. Behic was astute and he knew that developing friendships could prove to be expedient.

At the outset of the war, the Turkish Embassy in Paris began sending a significant number of missives to the

Ministry of Foreign Affairs in Ankara, Turkey's capital, but timely replies containing useful information were infrequent, often causing awkward situations.   WhenAmerican Ambassador Bullitt telephoned Behiç to convey his congratulations on October 19, 1939, Behiç was caught off guard and asked why he was being congratulated. From Bullitt he learned that a Non-Aggression Pact had just been signed between Turkey, England, and France. Although he was surprised and embarrassed because he had not learned about this from Ankara, Behic regained his composure as other congratulatory calls followed. In fact, Ankara never did inform the Turkish embassy of this treaty. When the Turkish General Secretary of the Foreign Affairs Numan Menemencioğlu arrived in Paris to draft an economic cooperation agreement the following month, Behiç explained to him the awkwardness of such a situation.

Numan replied indifferently that it must have been an oversight. This caused Behic to worry. An oversight is when you forget to tell the ambassador that the president's residence had been redecorated, not when you forget to tell him that the country he is representing just signed a wartime treaty! Should the flow of information, which was obviously poor, become worse as war spread over Europe, the result might be that the Turkish Embassy could become more isolated from Ankara, especially with the Nazis only a few hundred kilometers from Paris.

THE JEWS IN FRANCE

* * *

On 16 May 1940, France was in panic. Prime Minister Paul Reynaud's Chargé d'Affaires telephoned the Turkish Embassy that morning to inform Behiç that there was a strong possibility the German Army was going to enter Paris that evening and suggested the Turkish embassy staff should make preparations to leave Paris. Although later that day the German Army veered off towards the English Channel and the march into Paris was postponed for a while, Behiç requested a meeting and went to see Prime Minister Paul Reynaud at 7:30 p.m. on 17 May. The scene he encountered was extremely depressing.

"What's the latest situation?" Behiç asked the Prime Minister, who was visibly shaking.

"Although it's very dangerous, it's not completely hopeless," he replied, still shaking.

On May 24, Behiç visited the American embassy and had a private meeting with Ambassador Bullitt. While talking with the ambassador, Behiç saw workers piling sandbags in front of all the embassy windows.

Using a map that was spread out over his conference table, Ambassador Bullitt showed Behiç that the Germans had left a 30-kilometer gap around the city. Knowing Behiç was a former army commander, Bullitt sought the Turkish ambassador's thoughts on the German's intentions. Paris would be at the mercy of the Germans very soon and it was obvious to a military strategist like Behiç that the moving of French Government to safer ground was imminent. Therefore, it was time to make the preparations that would allow him to close down the Embassy and to vacate Paris at a moment's notice. He was sure it was a matter of days before an official communication from Ankara would arrive instructing him to do just that.

An incredible wave of bombing began just as Behiç sat down to lunch at 1:30 p.m. on June 3, 1940. All the windows of the embassy shook violently. The precinct police urged the Turkish diplomatic staff to move to the shelter they had prepared in a basement room beneath a seven-story building across the embassy; at the time all bomb shelters in France consisted of just basement floors. However, Behiç refused for he was used to the sound of bombs from the Balkan War and the War of Liberation. He knew from experience that the bombing was happening somewhere outside the city. With explosions edging closer, the bombing continued with an increasing intensity and lasted for forty minutes during which Behiç continued to eat without altering his composure. Later, it was discovered that one of the bombs had dropped a mere 300 meters from the embassy. The attack had been successful for the Germans. The two hundred planes had targeted and leveled the two most important factories in France, Renault and Citroen, and their vicinity, leaving more than 1,000 dead and 2,000 wounded in their wake.

Shortly after the bombing, a number of French Jews that were of Turkish descent arrived at the embassy. They were frantic that the French government would turn them over to the Germans. The immigration of Turkish Jews to France occurred during the final years of the Ottoman Empire.

Most of these immigrants had been the graduates of French schools, operated by the Paris-based Alliance Israélite Universelle, in the Ottoman Empire during the 19 century.

There were several factors that precipitated the emigration of Jews from the Empire. Many Jews left after Sultan Abdulhamid the Second, who resolutely upheld minority rights, was removed from the throne in 1909. No one knew if his successor would uphold the same privileges and respect for minorities as he had. There were also those Jews who had immigrated to France after hearing that the Greeks, who had advanced into Anatolia after invading Izmir in 1919, were slaughtering everyone in sight, Muslims and Jews alike. Another exodus of Jews occurred when the French Army vacated the country after the Turkish war of Liberation in 1923.

Before World War II all the French government knew was that there were slightly over 330,000 Jews living in France. No one was interested in their origins. Once the Germans became the puppet masters, they instructed the French government to conduct a census first to determine the number of French Jews in Paris who were over 15, then break it down to country of birth and/or descent. According to the census there were 113,467 French Jews of which 26,158 were of Polish descent, 7,298 were of Russian descent, 4,382 were of Romanian descent, 3,381 were of Turkish descent, 1,926 were of Hungarian descent, 1,703 were of German descent, and 1,642 were of Greek descent the majority of whom lived in the 11th Precinct, around Faubourg Saint Antoine.

The Turkish embassy in Paris took a headcount of their own and including Turkish Jews under the age of 15, they estimated that there were around 5,000 Turkish Jews in the metropolitan area and for the entire country they extrapolated the total number of Turkish Jews with French citizenship to be about 10,000, a number that was later officially confirmed.

Information obtained from records in the Paris Embassy and consulates around France, confirmed that there were 10,300 Jews who were Turkish citizens registered with Turkish authorities bringing the total number of Turkish Jews in France to about 20,000.The term "irregulars" was used to identify those Jews who had given up their Turkish citizenship to become French citizens and "regulars" for those who were still Turkish citizens.

The population census of Jews in the Unoccupied Zone extremely aggravated Behiç Erkin and he requested an audience with Field Marshal Pétain to express his discontent as well as to ask for Petain's help. He summarized the meeting in his memoirs which he said had turned out to be a monologue. Petain had listened without uttering a word, devoid of any facial expressions or body gestures that would convey his agreement or disagreement.

"Your Excellency, the Jewish Task Force conducted a population census in the Unoccupied Zone to which people from every region of France have immigrated since the beginning of the war. Naturally, during this migration Jews came to Vichy France to escape the Germans. Our embassy and consulates have made you aware that the majority of our Jewish citizens have immigrated here as well. Information gathered by the Jewish Task Force through this census could be very valuable to the Germans. I don't mean in terms of numbers, but in respect to details gathered it is quite valuable and if it were acquired by the Germans it could lead to perilous results. We both have experienced many wars. I was in and lived through the Balkan War, the Battle of the Dardanelles, World War I, and the War of Liberation and you are the famous hero of the Battle of Verdun. We both know very well that wars always end. However those who make grave mistakes during the war are held responsible for them after the war. Sharing the details of this list with the Germans may be one of those grave mistakes. This mistake will become a dark blemish for France and will remain as an indelible mistake in a history that boasts people like Emile Zola and Victor Hugo who are lauded for their contributions to humanity. The sin of placing these people in the hands of the Germans and enabling them to commit atrocities against these people will in no way be absolved in this life or in the afterlife. If the subject of sharing these details should surface, I implore you to prevent it from happening."

* * *

Article 88 in the 1923 Constitution of the Republic of Turkey stated the following regarding citizenship: "Everyone who resides continuously in Turkey is considered a Turkish citizen. Those living abroad can retain their citizenship for life, provided that they update their registration every year with the local consular office." Because so many Turks living abroad had the tendency to become citizens of their adopted countries, the law was amended in 1935. Those who had not registered nor been to Turkey during the War of Liberation or during the subsequent five-year period would lose their citizenship status. The amendment also increased the mandatory registration update period to five years. When the law was implemented, many people did register but as of 1940 there were quite a few Turkish Jews with French citizenship who had not felt the need to register and as a result lost their Turkish citizenship. So while approximately 10,000 Turkish citizens were registered as Jews, there were nearly another 10,000 who remained unregistered.

Realizing that as fear and panic spread throughout all the Jewish communities of France this situation could explode, head clerk Fatin Rüştü Zorlu went to the Ambassador to tell him of the situation and requested instructions. The response was immediate. Whoever could present an I.D., any document or title of deed issued either in the Ottoman Empire or the Republic of Turkey, could fill out a citizenship application form would instantaneously be granted citizenship affidavits.

"Sir, many do not speak a word of Turkish let alone have any papers. All they know is that some long-time ago, their parents, or grandparents lived in the Ottoman Empire!"

"Well, then, have them memorize the phrase '*I am Turkish; my relatives live on Turkish soil*' in Turkish and then grant them citizenship affidavits."

According to Zorlu, my grandfather then smiled mischievously and said, "Tell them not to worry. Germans don't understand Turkish."

The order then went out to all Turkish consulates in both occupied and in Vichy France that they were to issue citizenship affidavits to any Jew claiming his ancestors once lived in Turkey or in the Ottoman Empire and could utter that same phrase in Turkish. Most ambassadors would have sent communiqués to their governments asking for either directions or for the approval of plans but based on previous experience Erkin felt his messages would be ignored based on the fact that Inonu appointed him to make decisions on the spot. Eventually he would have to inform Ankara but now there were other pressing issues concerning the safety of his own staff.

On Sunday evening, June 9, France's former ambassador to Ankara called the Turkish embassy to inform Behiç what most people already knew. The French government had evacuated Paris that morning. He asked if the embassy could please send someone to the French Ministry of Foreign Affairs and pick up the official bulletin requesting all embassies to evacuate Paris because there was nobody left to make the delivery.

The plans and preparations for moving the embassy from Paris to Vichy had already been made and the time had come for implementation. Only three people from the staff were to remain to assist the Consul Chief Cevdet Dülger: 2nd Clerk Şevket Utkuman, a building supervisor, and a Swiss servant named Ernest. Dülger had actually wanted to leave Paris with the rest of the embassy staff but the ambassador decided it would be better if he remained to address the welfare of Turkish citizens in the metropolitan area.

Since there was an explicit written directive from Ankara to close down all diplomatic corps in Paris, Dülger was furious with Behiç's decision to keep the Consulate General open and have him stay in Paris.

Knowing the Germans as he did Behic was certain that they were going to be upset about his decisions regarding the Jews. The situation would become more difficult and increasingly dangerous. Behic wanted to take precautions and felt that the best thing was to send the spouses and children of the staff who weren't going to Vichy, back to Turkey. Behic then spoke to 3rd clerk Melih Esenbel and explained his concerns. Esenbel gathered the entire ambassadorial staff and informed them that the ambassador had ordered all wives and children of those remaining in Paris to return to Turkey. Since Vichy was unoccupied by the Germans it was considered safer so those going to Vichy were allowed could bring their families with them. Nobody was in a position to object to an order that came directly from Erkin. Behiç set out for Vichy with a 20-person entourage that included his undersecretary, chief clerk and spouse, second clerk, two third clerks and their spouses, military and vice-military attachés and their spouses, local clerks and other staff members.

On the night of June 11, Behic was awakened by a phone call from Prime Minister Paul Reynaud who told him that Italy had just announced it was going to declare war on France at midnight. In the face of this worsening situation the Prime Minister wanted to confirm

Turkey's friendship. The next day Behiç met with the French Secretary General of Foreign Affairs who, initially, behaved somewhat less than cordial because Turkey was still neutral. However, as François Charles-Roux spoke, he became visibly upset when he realized what war was going to cost his country. Attempting consolation, Behic reminded Charles-Roux that all nations including France had witnessed such conditions on a number of occasions throughout history. He also reminded him of the conditions that were forced on Turkey after the 1918 armistice. It took Turkey about five years to rise from ashes of that war. France, a richer country, would be able to bounce back much faster.

During their stop in the city of Tours on their way to Vichy on June 12, the French President, who chaired the Council of Ministers, explained to the rest of the government just how dire the military situation was. Regardless of a call for armistice, France would be unable to save herself entirely from German occupation. Behiç had been privy to this information even before Churchill had arrived at Tours for a scheduled briefing.

Behiç was apprehensive about the ambition, discipline and the no-holds-barred attitude of the Germans which he had seen firsthand during the last war. His instincts told him that wherever one fled during this war, one would eventually encounter the Germans. His June 12 entry into his memoirs had a hint of irony. "I didn't accept President □smet's proposal of ambassadorship to Berlin, and now look at the mess I'm in! I suppose no matter what I do, dealing with the Germans is my fate."

Field Marshal Pétain became the Prime Minister of the Vichy government and Pomaret was appointed his Interior Minister. Contacting both, right after their inaugurations, Behiç tried to gather information on the Germans. Paying the French Interior Minister a visit on June 23, he was surprised that Pomaret was in such a great mood, when in reality the situation was quite depressing. The French were about to sign an armistice with Germany. To Behic, it was obvious that Pomaret didn't know the Germans well.

The armistice was signed on June 25, 1940 at Compiegne, the spot chosen by Adolf Hitler because at that very place and in that very railcar, the Germans had been forced to sign the treaty declaring their defeat and capitulation on November 11, 1918. Hitler briefly boarded the railcar but quickly disembarked, leaving the generals to sign the treaty with France.

Even before the ink was dry on the ceasefire agreement, Germany had annexed a wide swath of territory encompassing Pas de Calais, Nord, and Alsace-Lorraine, creating a significant area of occupied France. What made matters worse was Article 18 of the treaty, which stated that the French Government was obligated to pay the expenses incurred by the occupying German forces initially estimated at six billion Francs per day, later reduced to four hundred million Francs per day. Article 19 of the treaty was sinister and cruel but had to be accepted by the French if there was to be peace. Article 19 stated that all refugees who fled from Germany to France had to be deported and sent back.

My grandfather Behiç assumed that Armistice Day, June 25, would be a day of national mourning in France, everyone staying indoors, French flags displayed everywhere at half mast, people going to church, fearful of the future. What he saw that day as he went to call on Monsieur Herriot, speaker of the French parliament, took him completely by surprise. People were out in the streets, at the cafes, leisurely walking along the promenades as if they didn't have a care in the world. Herriot behaved rudely, looking out the window rather than at the Ambassador and the rest of the Turkish delegation. He began to mutter and grumble under his breath, "They tricked me; they deceived me!"

"Pardon me, Monsieur Speaker, but who tricked you?"

Herriot suddenly wheeled around, shoved his red face about an inch away from the Ambassador's, and exploded, "You and the Russians!"

Quite calmly Behic asked how the deceit supposedly happened. The calmer he was the more furious Herriot became. He started screaming that Turkey had not entered the war after Italy jumped into the fray

"You were already contemplating a treaty with Italy when she entered the war. With whom were we supposed to have sided? I doubt anything would have been different for you even if America had entered the war."

Herriot looked as though he was going to tear the Ambassador to shreds. "Had you entered the war on our side, everything would have turned out differently."

THE FIRST JEW TO LEAVE

* * *

In 1492 and throughout the Inquisition many Spanish Jews had found asylum in Thessalonica thanks to the Ottoman Sultan Beyazid II. Aron Angel, the fourth child of Avram Albert Angel and Ester Levi Bivas was born in Istanbul in 1916. As a child, Avram Angel had moved with his family from Thessalonica to Istanbul in 1889. Aron's mother, Ester, had been born in Balat, the Jewish area of Istanbul. Like many Jewish children in Istanbul, Aron was educated at the Ortakoy Jewish primary school and the Jewish high school in Istanbul. During his senior year he also took courses at Galatasaray, the French high school.

Aron wanted to become an architect and study in France where his older sister, Bella, was a physician. Mentioning his goal to his geography teacher, Mr. Louat, who was French, Aron was told that he could introduce him to Prof. Henry Prost, a well-known architect and city planner whom he had recently met. Prost had designed the infrastructure for Antwerp, Belgium, as well as the Paris Regional Plan and the Istanbul Master Plan. Naturally, Aron jumped at the chance of meeting Prof. Prost the following day.

Aron forwarded the information he received from Henry Prost about the four universities in Paris with architecture departments to his sister Bella and asked her to decide which one would be the most suitable for him. Waiting for her reply, Aron enrolled at Istanbul Technical University and took courses there for one year. With help from her friends who were professors, Bella had chosen the Ecole

Speciale d'Architecture and scheduled an appointment for Aron to meet with the director. In the summer of 1937, Aron sailed from Istanbul to Marseilles on a ship called the Lamartine and then took the train to Paris.

A surprise was waiting for Aron when he walked into the director's office. Waiting to greet him was Professor Henry Prost! After examining Aron's school records Professor Prost explained to him that he could receive two years worth of credit for the courses he had taken at ITU providing he passed the exemption exam, which he did easily. Prof. Prost suggested that Aron take Urbanism (city planning) at Sorbonne University in addition to the full schedule at Ecole Speciale d'Architecture de Paris. Aron's classes began at 8:30 am and continued through the day to 5:30 pm with only one break for lunch. Besides, the Sorbonne was several kilometers away from the Ecole so it would be impossible.

Professor Prost, who was not only the director of Aron's university but the head of faculty at Sorbonne as well, told Aron that the metro covered the distance between the two universities in eight minutes, and that he himself would set the timing of the classes to accommodate Aron's schedule. Aron gladly accepted the offer. He was leading an extremely busy life but it was good.

* * *

That good life lasted for only two years. One day, Aron received a telephone call from the Turkish Embassy informing him that Ambassador Behic Erkin wanted to speak with him. This was an exciting moment for Aron. He had no idea why such a famous war hero would invite him to the embassy but he was thrilled. After arriving at the embassy, he was shown into the Ambassador's room where it was obvious that he wasn't the only guest. The room was full of other Turkish students.

Ambassador Erkin gave a brief account of the latest world developments. The German Army was only a few kilometers outside of Paris and it was only a matter of time before marched into the city. He also explained that one of the Parisian newspapers had published an article that day claiming Turkey entered the war against the Germans; but since the Ambassador had been unable to confirm this with Ankara, it was still unsubstantiated. Regardless, Behiç felt that for the time being it would be better if the Turkish students were moved to safer locations, away from the advancing Germans. Behiç gave the students an allowance for the road and sent them off to Bordeaux where housing had been arranged. He pulled Aron aside and told him the Germans would certainly detain him since he was Jewish. That's when Aron realized he was the only Jew in the group.

* * *

They stayed in Bordeaux for a few months until word arrived that all the students were to go to Paris because the Turkish Embassy had made arrangements for them to return to Turkey by train. Soon after his arrival in Paris, one of his friends remarked that the Germans were rounding up Jews in the Parc des Princes and it might be worth seeing. Since the Parc des Princes was just a few blocks from where he lived, Aron decided he could view it from a safe distance. Cautiously he made his way to the area and was confronted by an incredible sight. Germans soldiers were checking I.Ds and all Jews were being detained. Families were torn apart as men, women, and children were placed in separate holding areas. Mothers were crying for their babies; husbands were crying for their families; tearful children were calling for their parents. Treating the Jews like cattle, the soldiers shoved people on to busses and sent them away.

Aron found it difficult to comprehend the tragedy unfolding before him. These people were being treated like criminals and their only crime was being Jewish. Then, it struck him. That is what would happen to him, too, because he was Jewish. Petrified, he ran to the apartment he shared with his sister where he would be safe. Their apartment was in the 16th district of Paris. The building owned by Madame Labesse, a kind lady who provided room and board. Every night she brought Aron dinner and stayed for a chat keeping him company as he ate.

One evening, after setting down the food on the table, Madame Labesse showed him a document she was given by the Germans. It was a questionnaire with 50 questions designed to determine whether any Jews lived in a particular building. With a disgusted look on her face she commented to Aron, "as though I would let any of those disgusting Jews live under *my* roof."

Obviously Madame Labesse was unaware that Aron and his sister were Jewish. Aron was anxious to leave France realizing that no place would be safe in Paris. A few days later, after receiving the necessary information from the Consulate, he was on the train bound for Istanbul with ten other Turkish students. There was no trouble during the trip because thanks to the foresight of Behiç Erkin, the Turkish Consulate changed Aron's name to Harun on the passenger list given to the Germans. In the autumn of 1940, Aron, the first Jew rescued by Ambassador Behiç Erkin, was back in Istanbul.

From his memoirs, it is quite evident that my grandfather took nearly every opportunity to discuss the predicament in which all French Jews now found themselves. He wanted to know what the other embassies and their legations were going to do to help their Jews who were now in France. While Ambassador Erkin was working to protect his own Jewish citizens, the American Embassy sent a diplomatic note to the Turkish Consulate-General, stating us that the United States of America felt that these laws didn't differentiate between Jews and that it suggested its own citizens to accept these laws:

The Embassy of the United States of America, Paris
17 October, 1940

To the Consul-General of the Republic of Turkey,

To my esteemed colleagues,

Please accept my apologies for my belated response to you regarding the registration of property owned by German Jews. Nowadays, I'm informing American citizens who apply at our Embassy that they are voluntarily obliged to abide to the laws as U.S. citizens living in France. However, we can take the initiative whenever there is any discrimination. As far as we can tell, no discrimination is being practiced whereas it is applied on all members of the Jewish faith residing within occupied territory. I would greatly appreciate hearing from those who have opinions that are to the contrary.*

Mynard B. Barnes, 1ˢᵗ Ambassadorial Secretary

DEATH'S APPROACHING FOOTSTEPS

* * *

On October 23, 1940, Deputy Prime Minister of France Pierre Laval[2] met Hitler at Montoire-sur-Loire and the French-German partnership began.

It took a little while for the French to get things going because of all the political infighting. On December13, Pétain, in a shrewd political move, forced Laval to resign from power. He wouldn't even allow Laval to enter the Park Hotel, the Vichy government headquarters, to collect his personal things. Instead Laval was placed under house arrest at his home in Chateldon, located 15 kilometers outside of Vichy. With Laval out of the way, Pétain announced his decision to remove him from the government and sent a telegraph to Hitler assuring him that the policies originally negotiated between their two governments would hold. He explained that the reason for Laval's dismissal was the fundamental incompatibility between the two of them.

* * *

On July 11, 1940, Affairs Undersecretary Charles-Roux invited Ambassador Behiç to meet with him at his office in the Park Hotel, the Vichy government headquarters.

---

2   Laval was a French politician, four times President of the council of min-isters of the Third Republic. Following France's Armistice with Germany in 1940, he served twice in the Vichy Regime as head of government, signing orders permitting the deportation of foreign Jews from French soil to the death camps. After Liberation (1945), he was arrested, found guilty of high treason, and executed by firing squad.

Grandpa Behiç entered the chaotic lobby and headed towards elevators but he was halted by a guard. Pointing to an officer behind a small desk, the guard told Behiç he had to sign a request form stating who he wanted to see and the reason for his visit. Then, if his request was accepted, he would be allowed to go upstairs. These directions might have intimated others but not Behic Erkin who looked directly at the guard and mincing no words gave his reply. "I don't have any business here. I was invited by Undersecretary Charles-Roux and now I am leaving. If you like, you can tell him that the ambassador of Turkey was here and you did not let him go upstairs." Not waiting for a retort, he turned and walked out of the building.

He hadn't been back at the embassy very long when Behic received an apologetic phone call from the Roux's office. He was asked to return at 5 pm. After the way he had been treated, Behic said that another visit was out of the question. The caller assured him that an official would be waiting for him at the door to take him upstairs.

Returning at 5 p.m. Behiç met with Charles-Roux who informed him that he would like to meet with the Ambassador on a weekly basis regardless of having business to discuss because he felt these meetings would be beneficial for them both. Behiç was adamant. "If we are not allowed to come and go freely, I will never again set foot in this building!"

The French knew that the Turkish Ambassdor Behiç was uncompromising. They resolved the issue by presenting Behiç with a colorful pass that would allow him access to the Park Hotel insuring that he wouldn't face such problems in the future. His point made, Behic accepted the offer to meet regularly.

As a part of his duties Charles-Roux submitted reports on the foreign embassies in France, including his weekly meetings with the Turkish Ambassador, to the newly appointed Foreign Minister, Paul Baudoin. Baudoin never received ambassadors but he was intrigued by Behiç and breaking tradition, invited him to the Chanteclair Restaurant next to the Park Hotel on August 31, 1940. Behiç accepted the invitation and reciprocated by inviting Baudoin to the Turkish embassy on September 18. Knowing that good relations would be invaluable, he developed excellent dialogues with Charles-Roux and Baudoin.

* * *

Nine days after the meeting with Baudoin at the embassy, the German Military authorities "requested" that the French Interior Ministry conduct a census of Jews and began issuing edicts in rapid succession regarding the Jewish populace in occupied France. On October 16, the French newspapers announced a new law entitled, "The Status of The Jews" was in effect. According to this law all Jews, except those who had received the *Legion d'Honneur* or other medals and military honors, were prohibited from working as civil servants, teachers, and officers.

Two days later, another edict ordered Jews to register themselves and their homes with the authorities and remain at home unless they had permission to leave. Anyone going to the unoccupied zone would not be allowed to return. The decree also stated that Jews could no longer deal in commerce and had to surrender the management of their businesses to Christians and to posting a visible sign in French and German that it was a Jewish Establishment.

The transfer of businesses was supervised by Dr. Kurt Blanke, the chief economic relations official in the Department of Jews . The stated intentions were that the businesses would be sold, usually for a devalued price, and the revenue deposited in a fund called *Caisse des Depots et Consignations* in the name of former Jewish owners although the Jews would not be able to touch the principal. Instead, they would be paid 2.5% yearly interest.

On October 12, 1940 Otto von Stulpnagel of the German Army Command in Occupied France sent out the following Notice.

Instructions for Temporary Administrators of Jewish Businesses.

The priority of the Temporary Administrators of the Jewish businesses is to destroy all valid documents that will allow Jews to contribute to the French economy. This way the French economy will not be derailed and the employees of these businesses will continue working by only servicing French and German patrons.

Temporary Administrators are responsible from ensuring that no Jews, even the prior owners of the establishment, have any control over the operation of the business. In case of emergencies, Jews may withdraw money from the business; however Temporary Administrators must be diligent to ensure that an impression that Jews have any authority is not created.

The Jewish employees will be terminated once the establishment becomes operational without the need for them. The administrators should never forget that their position is temporary and the ultimate disposition of the establishments will be carried out as soon as possible.

Once the need for Jewish employees is eliminated business can be disposed of in three ways:

1- Jews can either sell their enterprises or transfer their rights to non-Jews. This method is preferable since no time will be lost. However, the administrators must ensure that the purchaser is not influenced by the Jews. If there is doubt and it turns out the new owner is just a figurehead for the Jews through another agreement or allows Jews to assume their former position through a different scheme, all agreements will become null and void. When a contract is executed the relevant ministry will be informed at once and suspected agreements will be deemed void.

2-   If a Jew refuses to sell or hand over his establishment, as will be the majority of cases, Temporary Administrators have the authority to sell the said business to non-Jews either in its entirety or in parts. Contracts of such sales are to be immediately brought to the military headquarters. This is the most expedient way of achieving the transfer of an enterprise. In competitive fields, Jewish enterprises must be sold to non-Jewish competitors.

3-   Some of the enterprises may be redundant or not important for the French economy. These must be liquidated immediately by inventory sales executed either en masse or one at a time. In these enterprises inventory sales must commence without the procurement of new goods.

Redundant enterprises will be submitted to military headquarters for approval. After four weeks, all Temporary Administrators shall submit reports and those who are unsuccessful will be dismissed.

Temporary Administrators bear no responsibility towards the previous owners.

* * *

The arrival of the Germans not only split France into two as Occupied France under German administration and Unoccupied France under French administration in Vichy but reminded thousands of Jews, now French citizens, that they had once been citizens of the Ottoman Empire and the Turkish Republic. Seeking protection, they began arriving at the Turkish diplomatic offices in droves. The instructions issued by my grandfather were clear. All applicants claiming to have been a Turkish or Ottoman citizen

would be furnished with a citizenship affidavit. Behic believed that this would offer them protection.

Escape for Jews from the Germans to the unoccupied
regions proved to be futile. Outdoing the Germans, the
Vichy Government immediately implemented German
laws regarding Jews making them more stringent, a fact
Behiç found very disconcerting. Never had he imagined
that the German laws in occupied France as well as the
actions of the Vichy Government would lead to the confiscation of peoples' possessions, money, and even their businesses. Adding to the situation, under orders from Germany
the French banks announced that the accounts of those
customers who failed to provide proof of religion would be
confiscated. The Germans then opened all Jewish-owned
vaults in every bank confiscating all their contents.

In his memoirs, Grandpa Behic wrote that these awful
events reminded him of a meeting he had on July 29 with
Laval who was Deputy Prime Minister at the time. Laval clearly stated his belief that in order for the peace to exist in
Europe and for France to keep its independence, England
had to be defeated. Only Germany was capable of doing
that. While the sun continued to shine on the British Empire,
it would be impossible for France to maintain her independence. Therefore, Laval said he would assist the Germans
by all means possible.

It was that phrase, "by all means", that caught in Behiç's
mind making it clear that the situation for Jews in France
was dire. Jewish businesses in Paris could be shut down by
the Germans without a reason or advance notice. Soon
the German authorities began rounding up foreign Jews
including a few Turkish Jews. Just. Keeping a close eye
on the developing events, Behiç contacted the recently
appointed Foreign Minister, Pierre-Etienne Flandin, requesting a meeting to discuss the Ambassador's concerns.

When the victim was a Turkish Jew and if that person was able to send a message to the Turkish diplomatic corps, the Consulate would immediately send letters of protest and request the German and French authorities to unseal the business or the property. These requests were not only submitted to Ambassador Abetz, who was the representative of Adolf Eichman in France, but to the Chief of German Security Police in France Theodor Dannecker, replaced by Heinz Röthke in 1942, and to the head of German Information Bureau, Dr. Schmitt. If a reply had not been received in a month, the efforts were intensified. A Consulate official would personally visit the bureaucrats with documentation proving the Turkish citizenship of the victim and have the property returned to its rightful owner or have the victim released from detention.

In some instances French authorities blamed the Germans claiming that all the procedural formalities were not only because of the occupying authorities but were their responsibilities as well. Locating the correct party was difficult, explaining the situation was even more so! Time was critical and the Turkish diplomats had not a second to waste. The Jews of Turkish descent had no choice but to trust the Turkish diplomats whose jobs were exceedingly difficult and made worse when facing an uncompromising Nazi officer or a pro-German Frenchman. There were so many complaints lodged that a form letter was created.

Turkish Consulate-General, Paris, no. 605

In the light that Turkish laws do not discriminate against citizens based on religion, Turkish Consulate-General in Paris respectfully requests from the German Embassy to give the necessary instructions to all pertinent divisions in reference to the edict dated 18 October 1940, which has begun to impact the properties of Turkish citizens.

* * *

When Ambassador Erkin's tour of duty concluded at the end of 1940, President İnönü asked him if he would like to extend his current tour of duty for another year. A simple, concise, unhesitating 'yes' was the reply. There would be no respite for the Turkish legation as the Nazis began their systematic expulsion of the Jews from France.

Between August 20 and 25 of 1941, German soldiers began rounding up Jews in Paris and sending them to concentration camps. French Jews were the first Jews transported to Auschwitz for extermination.

A French organization named the Study Institute of the Jewish Question (d'Etude des Questions Juives), established in September 1941, began an anti-Jewish propaganda campaign in a monthly publication, *The Jewish Ledger* (Le Cahier Juive). The same organization began a series of anti-Semitic exhibits in Paris on September 5.

VICHY 1940-1941

* * *

My grandfather had to work with the new laws and decrees the Vichy Government, now a puppet of the Germans, was implementing. The juggling act, otherwise known as the job of the Turkish legation, continued as the edict concerning the disposition of Jewish establishments was implemented in full force. On November 20, 1940, a communiqué from the Ambassador was sent to the Ministry of Foreign Affairs in Ankara explaining the situation and suggesting the steps necessary to help the Turkish Jews in France. Partly because of his manner and partly because of the break in communications with Ankara, my grandfather conveyed his instructions to his subordinates without waiting for a reply or an approval. Behiç pointed out that people must comply with the law; however, if any Turkish citizen suffered financial hardship because of these new laws, Cevdet Dülger was to inform the relevant German and French agencies immediately. He also explained that every Turkish Jew must hang a sign on his or her business or house declaring he or she is Turkish! Behiç had also instructed all his consulates that they should try to resolve all Jewish issues through personal meetings with the German authorities instead of letters or communiqués.

The following Memo No.603 dated 12. 28. 1940 was sent to Consul-General Cevdet in Paris from the embassy in Vichy.

"Please arrange a meeting with the German authorities in reference to the abolishment of the intrusion into

the establishments of Turkish Citizens as per edict dated 18 November."

On December 31, 1940, Ambassador Erkin received a letter from Binyamin Kastro. In the letter Kastro recounted in detail the behavior to which he had been subjected in conjunction with his business and asked for Behiç's assistance. He also mentioned that the Turkish government protected all its citizens without discrimination, regardless of religious and that he was confident Behiç would rectify the injustice being carried out against a Turkish Citizen. Behic did not reply immediately. He was going to use his diplomatic social obligations as a means to an end.

There were sixty-one foreign embassies in Paris in 1939 but by the time Field Marshal Pétain held a reception at the Pavillion de Sevigne on January 1 1941, only forty countries still had ambassadors that could attend the event. During the reception Petain maintained his customary aloofness and reservation but making a point to greet Grandpa Behic and invite him to lunch that week. Joining them were a few ministers including Foreign Minister Flandin. The need to maintain good relations with the top executives of France was imperative if the Turkish Embassy and its Consulates were to operate systematically and smoothly and Behiç used that opportunity to invite the Foreign Minister to the Embassy in February.

* * *

When Behic replied to Kastro on January 8, he was able to state with a bit more confidence,

"Our Consul-General in Paris has been in negotiations for the exemption of Jews with Turkish citizenship from the edict issued by the occupation forces regarding Jewish businesses."

Communication No. 61 dated February 6, 1941, informed Ambassador Erkin that the Consul-General had a meeting with German authorities per the Ambassador's instructions, This meeting resulted in the dismissal of the temporary business administrators who had been assigned to the Jewish Turks' establishments. Now that two months had passed, the French declared that there would no longer be exceptions for any Jew based on nationality. As a matter of fact the Consul-General had learned from the Turkish citizens who had initially lodged complaints at the Consulate that the custodians were back. Apparently, the Germans had made their final decision. The letter ended with the Consul-General requesting further instructions.

The following week, Behiç received a handwritten letter from a Turkish-Jewish citizen named Mr. Albala. The well-written letter conveyed how frightened and confused Mr. Albala was.

On the one hand he had seen the punishment endured by those who had refused to comply with the laws and on the other hand he was hesitant about complying with he law because he did not want to hand over all his earthly goods to the authorities who might not hand them back. While Albala was quite aware of the delicate and risky nature of the situation, the letter showed that in his state of mind it was possible he could do something regrettable. Something regrettable would have an impact that went beyond one individual. There were three distinct threatening entities that would not hesitate to use "something regrettable" to their advantages: the authorities of occupied France; the occupying German authorities; and the Vichy government. One misstep by one misguided Turkish Jew could make it impossible for the Turkish embassy to help the rest of the Turkish Jews. Behiç immediately sent a reply to Mr. Albala before the latter did anything foolish.

Dear Mr. Albala,
I have received your letter. As you mentioned, our laws do not discriminate against our citizens based on religion or race. We have duly informed the French government of this fact. However, the French government is of the opinion that all foreigners residing in their country have accepted the current and future laws beforehand. At the moment negotiations are ongoing between the two countries.

My advice to you is that it is appropriate for you to provide the French officials with the requested information.

Until agreement is reached between the two countries, upholding the French laws would make it easier for us to defend our position.

My kindest regards,
The Turkish Ambassador to Paris

In his memoirs, Grandfather wrote that on March 3, 1941, he sent a report to Ankara titled *The Jewish Affair*, and was intended as a supplement to Communiqué No: 502/228 which had been written and sent on November 20. Though once again he asked for instructions, he really did not expect an answer and anyway he had no time to waste waiting for it. The developments felt eerily similar to his experiences in Turkey's War of Liberation. In 1920 the British Occupation Forces in Istanbul had issued a list of individuals to be arrested. The list which Mustafa Kemal sent to Behic contained many names among which were General Mustafa Kemal, Colonel İsmet (İnönü) and Colonel Behiç (Erkin). While Behiç was busy facilitating the escape to Ankara of those on the list, the English began a door-to-door search for him. Eventually he, too, escaped from the city and as soon as he had made his way to Bursa, word from Mustafa Kemal arrived asking Behiç to meet him in Ankara.

Once in Ankara Behiç was offered a choice of assuming two positions: Deputy Chief of Staff or Director of Railways. Although both positions were appealing, he had already made up his mind when Mustafa Kemal told him "I know how to win a war but I don't know how to get the army to the front. Unless you are in charge of railroads and the logistics, we will lose this war."

Behic agreed to take the position as long as no one, not even Mustafa Kemal interfered with his work. The logistics of transporting an army was the least of his problems. The length of available track was only a few hundred meters and the occupation forces were torching all the railroad equipment when they had the chance. Ninety-five percent of his workers were non- Muslim and the rumor that the parliament was planning to dismiss them all was spreading like wildfire. Behiç immediately rushed to Ankara, interrupted a ministerial meeting that Mustafa Kemal was attending and explained the situation. Yes, the majority of the railroad workers were non-Muslim, but they had established their allegiance by remaining while the traitors among them had already defected to the enemy. To punish these people for the crimes of others would not only be wrong but replacing them with inexperienced Muslims would reqire time for training and would compromise his planned logistics. Behic said that if the ministers were determined to dismiss the non-Muslim workers, he would resign.

What he did for the non-Muslim railroad workers in 1920 had to be done for the Jews in 1940. The first he had to meet with his diplomatic staff to explain his plan. He had to assure the personnel that the plan would work so they would not become demoralized and lose sight of their mission. He needed to use the diplomatic arsenal he was given to its best advantage so he called a meeting of his staff.

"Giving up is not an option. If the Germans lock the embassy doors, we'll get in through windows. If they shut the windows, we'll get in using the chimney. If they block that off, we'll dig a tunnel but we are never going to give up and they know it very well. Everyone is cautious when dealing with those who defend their beliefs to the end. Understand that this is a war of diplomacy. Whenever they say "No," we'll just change the wording and hit them again and again until we get what we want. Be aware of these balances because they are of the utmost importance. Looking at things from the German perspective we may think they will refuse our requests; but as long as Turkey maintains neutrality, I believe they the Germans will have no choice but to remain sensitive towards our insistent demands. The same does not hold true for the French because they have options. They may do whatever the Germans tell them to do or mirror the Germans to show them that they are more German than the Germans. On the other hand France would like Turkey to remain friendly since we are the most important neutral country so I don't see how they could refuse. In the unlikely event the French do refuse us, I am hoping to reach our goal by pushing my high-level contacts. So, don't ever worry. If the doors are slammed in your face while you're dealing with the details, don't lose sight of the big picture and remember the precarious balances I've been talking about. And remember, you are representing the Republic of Turkey."

Finishing his speech, Behic knew that his army was prepared for battle. The work of the Turkish diplomatic corps had begun.

After countless meetings with and objections by the Germans, the Turkish Embassy received a communiqué on February 28 1941 signed by Otto Abetz, Adolf Eichmann's representative in France.

The German Embassy, Paris, No.1331, to the Turkish Consulate-General in Paris, 28 February 1941.

In reference to your query dated 28 December 1940 No. 605, the German Embassy announces with all respect:

Edicts regarding measures taken against the Jews in conjunction with the French government that were issued by our army command in France, were developed in accordance with public safety and other demands. Authorities are not permitted to use initiative and these laws supersede any other decree and will be enforced to each and every denizen of France regardless of his/her nationality. However, the German Embassy will be willing to evaluate submissions in compliance with the regulations by the Turkish Consulate-General regarding individual cases of Jewish enterprises owned by Turkish citizens.

This was a remarkable concession by the Germans. It meant that Germany's upper echelon officially accepted the fact that Turkish Jews could be exempted. This in itself was an historical event. Ambassador Erkin and his Turkish diplomats had won a battle for the rights of Turkish Jews. With this victory under their collective belts, the Turkish delegation became even more committed to the Ambassador and his plan. Behiç had been right. In the face of their insistent demands for the rights of Turkish citizens the Germans could not risk opposing the Turks. Morale was at a new high and the prevailing, optimistic attitude was one of determination to win this war within the war. Behiç listened with an amused smile as his undersecretary conveyed the newfound confidence of the staff.

"This is just the beginning. I worked with the Germans for four years while in the Ottoman Army. Who knows what they will hit us with in the days ahead. Remain composed no matter what happens and don't allow a negative attitude to demoralize anyone."

In March 1941, Xavier Vallat was appointed as the Commissioner-General for the Jewish Question (hereafter referred to as the Jewish Task Force) with an office in the Hotel d'Alger in Vichy. As the mastermind behind the anti-Semitic smear campaign against the former Jewish Prime Minister Leon Blum in 1936, Xavier Vallat was well qualified for the position. He was an energetic man determined to prove to the Germans that the French could implement and execute the anti-Jewish laws better and more successfully than the clumsy occupation forces. His agenda was to be given full command and authority over Jews in both the Occupied and Unoccupied zones.

Vallat's first order of business was to meet with Nazi General Otto von Stülpnagel at the Hotel Majestic in Paris on April 4. There he learned that the Germans were planning to begin purging Jews from the occupied territories and asked whether Vallat would be willing to assist in jailing or banishing all Jews, especially those with foreign passports, from the occupied lands. Vallat told him that while mass arrest was the job of the police controlled by the Germans, the forced emigration of Jewish refugees by the thousands from the Occupied France to the Unoccupied Zone was the decision of the Vichy Government. Hearing this, the Germans wanted to know if Vallat could ensure that Jews would be completely removed from the French economy as soon as possible. It was easy to agree since Vallat had already been given the same task by Field Marshal Pétain.

The General's civilian aide, Dr. Werner Best, had attended the meeting and was disappointed with Vallat whom he expected to be more aggressive. On some aspects Vallat hadn't appeared as eager as a Nazi would have been which wasn't all that surprising.   While   Vallat planned to confiscate virtually everything the Jews owned, including their money, property, businesses, factories, houses, and cars, and transfer it all to the French state, the Germans were planning to deport all Jews with foreign passports from the occupied territories and implement the Final Solution.

Eager to prove his worth to the Germans, Vallat wanted to expand the scope of the laws against Jews as fast as possible. With the new law for the Unoccupied Zone in his pocket, Vallat proposed an extremely detailed census be made on the Jews. In addition to the names of children, spouses, mothers, fathers, grandfathers, and grandmothers; information on education, military service, possessions, and properties, personal and business-related debts would be included.

On May 15, 1941, Undersecretary Zeki gave Behiç a report sent by Consul-General Cevdet Dulger in Paris. French authorities had rounded up approximately 4,000 Jews living in Paris and had shipped them off to concentration camps. The majority of these were citizens of Poland, Czechoslovakia, and Austria, countries under German occupation. Among these thousands of Jews there was one Turkish Jew. Behic was about to jump on that fact when, reading on, he saw that Cevdet had secured this Turkish Jew's release by contacting the French police and the French had issued some sort of an apology by admitting it had been a mistake. "Now the French are beginning to show their true colors. Zeki, notify our consulates in Lyon and Marseilles; let them know what happened in Paris; it'll cheer them up a bit."

Remembering Ankara's order to close down the Consulate-General in Paris he added, "If I had obeyed the order God knows what would have happened to my fellow citizens. From now on we need to be even more diligent!" he said. There were still Turkish Jews in Paris who needed protection.

To facilitate and speed up the confiscation of Jewish properties in both Occupied and Unoccupied France, a separate property census was taken in June. It seemed to Behiç that not only the French police, but practically the entire French population suddenly accepted the theory of the Vichy Government which laid the blame on Jews for the collapse of France. The French had turned against the Jews. Turkish Jews throughout France were becoming more and more anxious not only because of the property census but because of the way they were being treated. As a result they began streaming into the Turkish Embassy and Consulates in unprecedented numbers.

On July 12, the head of the secretary-general for the police in the Ministry of the Interior, Henri Chavin, sent a memorandum to all precincts. "As a matter of public security, this census is of crucial importance; therefore, it is imperative that you concentrate fully and work with utmost care and diligence."

The police from all municipalities took part in the census and all Jews were counted regardless of their nationality. However, the Turkish Ambassador had no intention of letting Jews bearing identification having a Crescent and a Star succumb to practices created by Vallat. This would be another battle in the war within a war.

Also in July, the Consulate-General at Marseilles sent Communiqué No. 372/65 to the embassy reporting reported that they were encountering a steadily increasing number of Turkish Jews asking what to do in the face of the newly issued laws. The reply was the following:

1)   Regarding measures implemented by the French Government against Jews in Free France, we protect the rights of our Jewish citizens.
2)   In any event, in order to prevent actual losses to our citizens, a custodian will be appointed for their establishments by our Embassy.
Our initiatives regarding the first article are ongoing. I request that you notify me if there is any obstacle preventing you from implementing the second article.

Not only did Grandpa Behiç have to work with and around the Germans, the French under German occupation, and the Vichy government, he had to advise his own Consulates as well. Even though his directives were quite clear, both the Paris and Marseilles Consulates asked the ambassador what to do whenever the slightest amendment was made. The answer remained the same: "The general outline remains the same: Assistance will be rushed to every Turkish citizen living in France, regardless of their religion."

* * *

On August 12, 1941, a newly constructed apartment complex in Drancy, a suburb of Paris, was transformed into a concentration camp by the Germans. It was to serve as a holding station for Jews of foreign nationalities before their transport to Eastern Europe. Soon, however, native French Jews including two brothers of the former French Prime Minister Leon Blum, and from 1943 onward Turkish Jews were imprisoned there as well.

Theodor Dannecker, Chief of Gestapo's 4th Service Section was the first commander of this concentration camp which was manned by the SS.. However, in occupied France he was known as the *Judenreferat* (Jewish

Specialist). In July of 1942 Dannecker was replaced by Heinz Röthke, who commanded the camp until the end of 1943. Finally Alois Brunner became the commander who was most loyal to Hitler's Final Solution of the Jews and the most terrifying commander of the camp in Drancy.

The Jews being processed in Drancy Camp were divided. The French Jews, for some reason, believed they would be released and as a result belittled all other Jews as though it was the foreign Jews' fault that they were imprisoned. However, in the end all Jews suffered the same fate except for some of the Turkish Jews. Those few that survived Drancy reported that that the French guards stationed outside the camp Drancy proved to be even more ruthless towards the new arrivals than the SS.

LAZARE ROUSSO[3]

* * *

Since Paris had been declared an open city by 1941, all bombings had ceased and except for the German soldiers, Nazi Flags, and midnight curfew, life continued as usual with cafés and cinemas packed to capacity as though everything was normal. Missing curfew meant a trip to a French police station for an ID check then an escort home by a police officer avoiding any confrontation by the Germans.

December 13, 1941 began like every other day for Moiz Rousso who followed his usual routine: up at 6 a.m., shower and shave, set the breakfast table, and wake up his son. Breakfast was the most pleasant part of the day for Moiz since his son, Robert Lazare, had recently turned 20. Naturally the young man spent a great deal of time with his friends so breakfast was about the only father and son time they shared.

Like most winter mornings, father reminded son to dress warmly and take his I.D. with him. As usual, son informed father he would be out with friends that evening, but would not be home late. The expressions, "I worry" and "Don't worry" were exchanged as they parted that day.

When Lazare left the subway at Franklin Roosevelt Station in the Champs-Elysées to meet his friends that evening, he unexpectedly encountered Nazi soldiers when he reached the avenue above. They surrounded the exit and were loudly demanding that everyone show their IDs.

---

3   This section is based on a 2006 interview with the author in Istanbul.

Although nervous, he remembered his father told him that he carried a Turkish I.D. card and if stopped, must mention that fact. The German noticed only the word "Jew" on the I.D. written in big red letters. As he was grabbed, Lazare began to protest that he was Turkish.

"You're a Jew and that's all that matters," said the German.

Objecting was a waste of time as the soldier kept shouting at him.

"I was ordered to bring in all Jews I found. You're a Jew, so shut up and move!"

Lazare was shoved into the back of a military jeep where another detainee had already been placed. Looking at each other, the young man slowly and cautiously spelled the word 'Jew' with his finger on his overcoat. They were sharing the same fate having committed no crime.

They drove for what seemed to be a long time until they arrived at some type of large German facility. The scene was apocalyptic. German soldiers yelled and screamed nonstop and any detainee who tried to ask questions was shouted down. It was incredibly noisy, and confusion reigned as thousands of people were being herded like cattle. Lazare was numb as he was pushed onto a bus which drove off as soon as it was filled. He looked around and saw that everyone was as scared, confused, and as clueless as he was. As they rode, all he could think about was his father, how worried he must be, and how there was no way to get any word sent to him. Suddenly, the bus came to a screeching halt. As soon as the doors opened he saw they were at a train station, possibly Gard du Nord, and the prodding began anew, this time the Germans were pushing people into train cars. In precision-like fashion, as soon as all the cars were filled, the trains began to move.

It was 11 p.m. Moiz stood by the window, partially hidden behind the curtain, and searched the street for a sign of Lazare for the hundredth time. Midnight came and went. Nothing moved except the German military police making regular rounds By 2 a.m. any bad feelings Moiz experienced earlier turned into panic. Maybe Lazre had been picked up by the French Police for missing the curfew and was being kept overnight at the station to teach him a lesson. He would go to the local police station first thing in the morning, have his son released, and all would be well. He held on to this fleeting hope even as his gut feelings told him the situation was much worse. Every passing minute was an eternity. He thought about his late wife Sara who would have been a great help to him right now.

One evening, when they still lived in Istanbul, Moiz Rousso had shared his thoughts with Sara about his business, their son, and their future. Turkey had not been immune to the effects of the worldwide depression and Moiz's business was failing with little hope of recovery. There were relatives in France were the economy was picking up and realizing that if they wanted to provide their only child, Lazare, with a better future, they had to leave Turkey and move to France.

The Rousso family settled in Paris in 1933 in the 14th District. Life was hard and Moiz worked long hours to provide for his family. Although their relatives who had moved to France between 1915 and 1924 had become French citizens, Moiz would not follow their example.

"I'm still a Turk regardless of the fact that I'm Jewish; I grew up and did my military duty in Turkey. I gained the experiences I use today while living there. For years, I earned my living in Turkey. What difference will it make if I'm French? Will I get taller?"

Moiz was proud of being Turkish and renewed the Rousso family registration at the Turkish Embassy every year without exception until 1935 when he was told he only had to renew his registration once every five years due to the new law on Turkish Citizenship. When the war began, he lost his beloved Sara and the situation for Jews became worse. Germans occupied Paris and issued their Jewish laws such as the word "JUIF" (Jew) had to be printed on the identification of all Jews. Since there would be fines and jail sentences for those who did not comply, Moiz Rousso went to the local police station and submitted his and Lazare's IDs.

The rumors that the Turkish Embassy was closing and moving to Vichy, only made matters worse. Leon Mandil was the point man for the Turkish Jewish community since he worked at the embassy. Normally, Leon was close mouthed about the embassy but he assured people that the Ambassador was going to keep the Consulate-General open for the needs of Turkish citizens living in the Paris area despite Ankara's explicit orders to close. Furthermore, he told the Turkish Jewish community that they were not to affix the yellow Star of David on their clothes and to contact the Consulate whenever a French supervisor tried to interfere in their businesses.

That was all well and good thought Moiz, but Lazare was somewhere in trouble; he prayed, asking God to watch over his son.

The train finally stopped well past midnight and the cacophony of German voices began in earnest. Lazare couldn't understand why the Germans kept on shouting since everyone appeared to be following their orders. Looking around the platform he realized there must have been hundreds, maybe even thousands of people on the train. As soon as one train left the station, another quickly pulled in.

The temperature had dropped several degrees during the journey and the longer he stood on the platform the colder it seemed to get. Lazare noticed the station sign. They were in Compiegne. Again more shouting and Lazare's group was marched to a compound consisting of a military barracks and several dormitories surrounded by barbed wire. His mind was a jumble of disjointed thoughts. He was a long way from Paris and he was trying to figure out how he was going to go home once they realized he was Turkish. Then he started thinking about his father and became a bundle of nerves.

He gave his name to a German soldier who wrote it down on a ledger then handed him a small metal plate inscribed with the number 3233, a soup bowl, a spoon, and a blanket.

"This is your number: 3233. From now on you are No. 3233. You are responsible for these items; sign here to declare you have taken possession."

Lazare went into the 25-person dormitory bare except for straw on the floor which he assumed was meant to be a bed. After a horrible night, everyone was awakened at five o'clock the next morning with more shouting. They were forced to run to the courtyard, lineup in rows, and wait. They stood for three hours in the bitter cold of winter with, no explanation as to why they were there. First one soldier took a head count, then another, and then it was back to standing and waiting. A group of German officers came into the courtyard, looked at the detainees in utter disgust, then left. Lazare was in agony. Under normal circumstances he was unable to stand still for very long and now, he had spent three hours on his feet in the freezing cold practically immobile.

Again, without an explanation the Jews were led into the canteen. Lazare realized he hadn't had anything to eat since breakfast with his father the day before. He was famished but when it was his turn at the counter, his hopes sunk to a new low. One single ladleful of some unidentifiable gunk was dropped into his bowl and he was given a half mug of coffee. The coffee was unlike anything he had tasted. For all he knew it could have been warm, diluted, brown shoe polish.

While Lazare was confronting his breakfast, his father was at the local police station where he learned that the Germans had rounded up some Jews at house searches and at road blocks all over Paris the day before.

"But we are Turkish citizens and when the anti-Jew laws came into effect our Consulate told me that because we are Turkish, there was absolutely nothing to worry about."

"Since you are Jewish, Monsieur, my advice to you is to call on your consulate."

That morning was only the second time in Moiz Rousso's life that he missed going to work. The first time was when he his wife died and he wasn't about to risk losing his remaining reason for living by going to work especially if the Germans had his son in a concentration camp.

When Moiz arrived the Consulate-General was closed. For an instant, he panicked until it dawned on him that it was still too early for the workday to begin. As he waited, Moiz paced briskly back and forth to keep himself from freezing. Some hours passed and he noticed a steady stream of people arriving at the consulate. As they all waited for the office to open, Moiz asked about their situations to learn if others were having similar problems. They were all Jewish, yes, but 'irregulars' who had come to obtain Turkish identification papers.

As soon as the Turkish Consulate-General opened, Moiz explained his situation. The first thing the officer on duty tried to do was calm him down explaining that these queries were too serious to be handled over the telephone and they had to follow a specific protocol. First, the Consulate-General had to write an official petition to the relevant authorities. The foreign officials only responded to official inquires and only after looking into the matter and doing the necessary research.

Written queries would be sent to the appropriate French and German authorities, the Jewish Task Force, and the German Embassy to find out whether they had any information regarding Lazare. After that they would have to wait for the replies from the various departments. If any information about Lazare arrived, a written inquiry would be sent to that bureau asking why he was detained, along with a demand for his release on the grounds that Lazare was a Turkish citizen. Then the interminable wait for a reply would begin.

For Lazare, the cruelty began every morning at 5:00 a.m. with a roll call lasting 3 hours in the freezing cold; then breakfast consisting of a mug of disgusting coffee. Then it was off to the task of unraveling the tangled barbed wire wound on huge wooden reels that were brought to the camp every day. Lunch was only a cup of soup. More barbed wire. On more than one occasion, German soldiers fired into the air as soon as more than two people were together unwinding the barbed wire in the courtyard. Congregating was forbidden. Dinner was 200 grams of dark bread served with a smidgen of margarine one night and a speck of jam the next.

Once they were forced to strip naked then taken to the showers. The Germans checked their hair for lice and then pushed them under the cold shower. Lazare had a difficult time determining which was colder, the air, or the water. During roll call some numbers would be called; those individuals would step forward, line up, and then be taken away. Those who were singled out were never seen again. Rumors began concerning the fate of those 'numbers'. The prevailing opinion was that they were taken outside and shot in front of the barbed wire. Actually, Lazare learned later that they were communists and they *were* shot rather than sent to another camp.

Through the detainee grapevine, Lazare learned he was the only Turk in the camp, a fact which at first gave him hope. He couldn't understand why it was taking the Germans so long to rectify an obvious mistake. Maybe his father died from grief so the authorities could not be notified. He stopped himself from thinking such hopeless thoughts and tried to believe his father was still alive and looking for him.

The detainees were given barely enough food to keep them alive and Lazare was experiencing insufferable hunger. They were hovering between life and death made worse by the daily torturous three-hour long roll call in the freezing cold. Subsequently the elderly and those who couldn't take the starvation and cold collapsed, their bodies taken away.

Lazare had always been slim but since he had been at the camp he had punched his third extra hole in his belt. It had been eight weeks since Lazare was brought to the Nazi camp. He now weighed 48 kilos, dreamed about candies, cakes and cookies, and suffered from chronic depression and the fear of dying from starvation. It looked to him like people were melting away right before his eyes. Like the others in the camp he uncoiled barbed wire by day and slept inside barbed wire by night.

At the end of Lazare's eighth week in the camp, his number was called during roll call one morning. Lazare was so numb from cold and hunger that it took a while for him to respond. Taking his meager belongings, he followed the soldier, as he had seen others whose numbers had been called, and entered a room where a young soldier sat at a table.

"3233, hand over your number plate!"

He handed it over.

"Your bowl!"

He handed it over.

"Your spoon!"

He handed it over.

"Your blanket!"

He handed it over.

"Sign here!"

He signed.

Typical German mentality, Lazare thought to himself. They make you sign for stuff just before they shoot you in the head! Suddenly, he couldn't move. He was frozen, not from fear but from grief as he realized that he was going to die without being able to see his father one last time. Then he heard the soldier yelling at him to move so without thinking, he walked outside in the direction he had seen the other "numbers" walk when they left the building.

"HALT!" yelled a German soldier. Lazare stopped. His breath caught in his throat. He stood waiting without even looking back.

The soldier grabbed him by the arm, pushed Lazare in a different direction while cursing under his breath. They entered another building, and went upstairs to the entrance of a room where Lazare was told to wait as the soldier went in. Moments later the door opened and Lazare was ordered into the room that had a huge red, black, and white Nazi flag on the wall and four German soldiers waiting there for him in the room. He was so scared that he wasn't even aware if he was holding his breath or breathing normally.

"Is your name Lazare?" asked one of the officers.

For one moment he wasn't sure if he should say yes or no, it's 3233.

"Are you Lazare Rousso?"

"Yes."

"Are you Turkish?".

"Yes."

"You should thank your God that you are. You are free to go!"

At first Lazare thought he must have heard incorrectly. Then he realized that the Nazis were playing with him. As soon as he turned to leave they would shoot him in the back. He wondered if he told them he liked it at the camp would they let him live?

"I said you are free to go, now get out of here!"

"Where should I go?" Lazare thought that if he asked questions he would live a few moments longer..

"To Paris!" replied the officer shouting angrily in German.

Lazare was desperately trying to think of a ways to extend his life because he was sure he was going to be gunned down before he reached the door. So he began to chatter away that he had no money so he couldn't get a train ticket and he wasn't in any shape to walk to Paris. At that point the officer screamed at one of the soldiers to get Lazare a train ticket and in a few moments a third class train ticket was shoved into his hand. Aha, he thought. They will shoot me and then pry the ticket loose from my fingers. Still stalling for time Lazare asked how he would escape another arrest? He certainly didn't want to return to the camp. The officer reached into a desk drawer and Lazare began praying silently as he waited for the inevitable bullet. When he heard the sound of a pen scratching across a piece of paper, he opened his eyes and saw the officer writing.

"Show this paper if you are ever detained again."

Thinking that the Germans were still playing a game, he looked at the note written in German and asked what it said.

"Get out! When you get to Paris, don't forget to thank the Turkish diplomats."

Lazare left the room went downstairs and out of the building escorted by a soldier. Reaching the main gate, the guards were told to "Let him out, he's a Turk."

Barely able to walk, Lazare stumbled away from the camp. He was frightened, hungry, and exhausted and had no idea which way to go. From behind he heard someone shout "Go straight, turn right and you'll come to the station!"

Then he heard rounds of ammunition being loaded into chambers and his legs froze. His mouth, however, did not. Having reached his emotional limit, Lazare shouted at the soldiers. "God damn you 3233 times!"

The soldiers just laughed.

Lazare forgot about his hunger, his exhaustion, and fear, as he clutched the German document and his third-class train ticket and began to run. His heart was beating out of his chest as he reached the end of the road and turned right without looking back. When he saw the train station ahead of him, he realized for the first time that he was truly free. Lazare collapsed to his knees right in front of the station.

Lazare Rousso was taken into custody by the Nazis on December 13, 1941 and released on February 6, 1942.[4]

Until the laws against the Jews were implemented, Behic had been working on forging connections in the Vichy government and the Ministry of Foreign Affairs. It was time to call in a few favors so he called Undersecretary Rochat and requested a meeting. Behic began the meeting with a rhetorical question: "Have you ever contemplated what would happen if I were to advise my government to treat the French living in our country the same way you treat my countrymen here?" After explaining how and why it was impossible in the current situation for him to do anything for his fellow Turks living in France,

---

4   As recounted to author in 2006 Lazare Rousso said "The fact that there was such a powerful and decisive ambassador heading the Consul-Generals in Paris and Marseilles was God's will."

he requested Rochat's assistance in identifying the best avenues to pursue in order to help them.

* * *

Autumn brought not only a change of seasons but a change in the treatment of the Jews. On September 18, 1941, Himmler who was *Reichskommissar fur die Festigug des Deutschen Volkstums* (Reich Commissar for the Strengthening of Germandom) wrote the following in a letter to *Wartheleand Gauleiteri*[5] Arthur Greiser:

"The Fuehrer orders that both the old Reich (German Empire) and the states under occupation are to be purged of Jews as quickly as possible, starting from the west and progressing towards the east."

The next month, four individuals met to determine the most efficient way of fulfilling their Fuehrer's request. Zyklon B (hydrogen cyanide) had already been tested on children in the early 1940's and since it was an effective rat poison, there was plenty available. Erhard Wetzel (Director of the Bureau of Nazi Party Racial Policy); Victor Brack (the Fuhrer's Chancellor and chief of the Extermination Program); Alfred Roenerg (Occupied East Land Reich Minister and Jewish Question Consultant) and SS- Lt. Col. Adolf Eichmann devised the following plan. Extermination centers had to be built at existing concentration camps. Constructed to resemble showers, they had to be large enough to "batch process" those who were to be eliminated. The "showers" would last 7 to 8 minutes and the corpses would have to be destroyed by means of incineration.

The number of facilities for mass executions by gas was increasing by the day. The camps at Kulmhof (Chelmno), north of Lodz in East Prussia and at Birkenau, part of the vast Auschwitz complex in Upper Silesia, former Polish territory

---

5   Governor of Wartheland, the Polish territory annexed to Germany in 1939.

incorporated into the Reich, were ready for use. Belzec, Sobibor, Majdanek and Treblinka soon joined the list. Once in place, the death factories had to be supplied with those the Reich had deemed unsuitable. Organization, logistics, and coordination were essential and the Nazis began to tighten the noose.

In October of 1941, the Vichy government ordered all foreign Jews to be confined to their homes after registering their addresses at a nearby police station or rounded up and placed in special detention camps. On October 23, 1941, Heinrich Himmler issued an order barring the defection of Jews from Germany and its occupied territories in conjunction with the arrest and transfer of Jews to Nazi concentration camps. Himmler also demanded that the French assist in arresting and deporting the Jews to the camps. Two days after Himmler's order was published, Undersecretary Zeki gave Behiç the sad news from Paris. The Germans had executed 117 prisoners, all of them Jewish. In a quiet, barely audible voice, Behic commented about how sad everything was. The Germans were repeating what they did in other occupied countries. Today it was 117. Who knows how many it will be tomorrow?

In November the Jewish Task Force ordered all administrators to confiscate all Jew owned businesses, factories, stores, houses and all property. These decrees marked the beginning of the round up of about 70,000 French Jews living in almost every part of France.

By the summer of 1942, all Jews between the ages of 18 and 55 who had no steady employment and had immigrated to France after December 1932 were forcibly sent to concentration camps. Out of the 70,000 who were sent to the east from Drancy, only 3,000 would return.

I JUST WANTED TO INFORM YOU

* * *

During this period there were many personnel changes in the Turkish Diplomatic corps. Cevdet Dülger, Consul-General at Paris from August, 1939 to April 1942 was replaced by Namık Kemal Yolga ,Vice-Consul-General for a brief period between April and July of 1942, then later with Fikret Şefik Özdoganci, who arrived from Ankara in July 1942 and assumed the duties of Consul-General until May 1945.

Bedi'i Arbel was Consul-General in Marseilles from April 1940 to June 1943. After the Germans occupied the Unoccupied Zone in 1942, this Consulate was transferred to Grenoble. Bedi'i Arbel was succeded by Fuad Carım from June 1943 to May 1945 and Necdet Kent was Vice-Consul from 1942 until 1944.

* * *

It was extremely difficult for Turks living in Europe to retain or regain their Turkish citizenship because many of the Turkish consulates closed when the war began. Thousands who had abandoned their Turkish citizenship applied to the remaining Turkish consulates to have their citizenship reinstated. Since the introduction of anti-Jewish measures, their only hope for survival were the Turkish legations.

At first, the Turkish Government was reluctant to help. Government officials and many Turkish citizens wondered why Turkey should risk going to war with the Nazis in order to help people who had fled Turkey during the years when the Republic was being formed. Ever since the early 1930s, most newspapers in Turkey were pro-German and in 1939 and 1940 every German victory was lauded in the Istanbul and Ankara press. Despite declaring itself neutral in the great world conflict, most Turkish citizens believed the government was sympathetic towards Germany.

The Turkish ambassador's actions of helping Jews who were not legal citizens of Turkey should have caused a great deal of consternation in Ankara. However, under the circumstances it the Turkish government feigned ignorance about what was happening in France. Ankara always took its time to reply to the Embassy knowing that Behiç Erkin, who had been given carte blanche to deal with the Germans, was at the helm,

Reports that arrived from Paris showed that the Ambassador had taken the necessary measures in every issue even sending a diplomatic note to the French government without seeking Ankara's approval just to expedite matters. Although he kept his ministry informed of what he was doing, Behiç never felt the need to ask Ankara for permission for anything he did, and when he did ask, it was out of courtesy. Besides, he knew Ankara purposely took too long to read and answer his reports. It took four months to receive Ankara's comments to Behiç's communications that usually began with, "I just wanted to inform you…"

* * *

Behiç issued Citizenship Affidavits instead of passports because there was a limited number of available Turkish passports saved as replacements for those who lost them while travelling. Using affidavits eliminated the risk of sending thousands of blank passports which Ankara probably would have refused to send fearing Turkey's neutrality might be questioned if a shipment of thousands of blank passports were discovered by the Germans.

As word got out that you could get a Turkish affidavit of citizenship if you could memorize the words that your relatives lived in Turkey and if you put up a sign at your business saying "This workplace belongs to a Turkish citizen" the Turkish embassy and consulates would defend you, the consulate became busier by the day.

After the war when he was interviewed, Vice-Consul Namık Kemal Yolga explained the difficulties they had. "A matter which took up a great deal of our time was the situation of our 'irregular' fellow citizens. Paris Consulate-General was responsible for Paris and its immediate vicinity, where most of the Turks in France lived. When the occupation authorities began persecuting, the 'irregular' Turkish citizens stormed into the Consulate-General, at first crowding into the Chancery on the second floor, then filling the staircases which led up from the entrance hall, with the latecomers backing onto the sidewalk along Boulevard Haussmann."

Vice-Consul Necdet Kent recounted similar conditions at the consulate in Marseilles:

"When the Nazis occupied Northern France, many Turkish Jews, and others as well, fled to unoccupied Vichy France, and therefore entered the our consulate's assigned territory. But once the Nazis occupied Southern France, things got much worse. Their first act was to load all the Jews they could capture into trucks and send them off to Germany. In response to complaints about this from Turkish citizens, we acted. If the status of the Turkish Jew applying for assistance to the Consulate was 'regular', a Citizenship Affidavit document was provided immediately. In addition, a sign to be displayed at their establishment proclaiming the owner and the business were under the protection of Turkey was supplied.

With this method we saved many people from the Nazis. At first, the Nazis left these Turkish citizens in peace. However, as time passed and Gestapo Chiefs changed,

Nazis' attitudes changed as well and their attacks became more frequent. At times we had to go to Gestapo head-quarters as many as three or four times a day to rescue our fellow citizens."

While no official orders requiring Turkish diplomats to specifically protect Jewish Turks from being harassed or persecuted in Nazi-occupied Europe were ever issued by Ankara, Behiç had instructed his ambassadorial staff thro-ughout France to provide as much protection as humanly possible for all Turkish citizens.

* * *

The Turkish Embassy continued its regular communica-tions with the relevant authorities while the staff worked behind the scenes. After all, proper diplomatic relations had to be maintained. One official diplomatic note that was sent to the Ministry of Foreign Affairs read:

"The Turkish Embassy would kindly like to inform your government's Foreign Ministry that the text of Law No.2333 published on 2 June, 1941 which orders Jews to register all their properties and assets or else face sig-nificant penalties gave us the impression that this law was applicable to Jews of Turkish citizenship living in France as well.

The Turkish government does not discriminate against its own citizens based on race, religion or for any other reason. Consequently the Turkish government is appre-hensive and concerned regarding the mandatory app-lication of these laws to its citizens of Jewish descent resi-ding in France. Therefore you are herby informed that we reserve our full rights with regards to our Jewish citizens."

A short while later came the reply from the Ministry of Foreign Affairs.

"The French Foreign Ministry wishes to kindly inform the Turkish Embassy that all those residing in France must unconditionally accept the laws of the host country. In accordance with this principle precautions taken in regards to those of Jewish ethnicity are applicable to French citizens as well as all foreign nationals without exception."

This response angered Behiç because now his initiatives to help his countrymen turned into a full-fledged diplomatic war. That was fine with him. Throughout his professional life, whether as a commander in the Liberation War or as the Minister of Public Works during the infancy of Turkish republic, my grandfather had overcome countless difficulties and adversities and had always persevered. In his memoirs he wrote that he had no intention of losing the diplomatic battle in France when the lives of thousands were at stake. He devised a new diplomatic assault which he believed would corner the French Government. This time he stated that the anti Jewish laws were a violation of the treaties between Turkey and France since these treaties clearly stated that Turkish citizens residing in France had the same rights as the French citizens living in Turkey. He concluded his communication with the following statement.

"As much as it is expected for foreigners to abide the laws of their adopted countries, in reference to the French Ministry of Foreign Affairs' view that foreigners must accept the current and future laws of the country they in which they reside, your answer to my inquiry should have been the following: You retain your rights in case we, the French government, discriminate against any Turkish citizen."

The more aggressive the Nazis became, the more creative the ambassador grew. The Germans began a circumcision check to detect Jewish men. As if that were not demeaning enough, it was done in the middle of the street in Paris in broad daylight. When word got back to the embassy, Behic formulated a plan. Since Muslims were also circumcised Jewish lives could be saved if they had a document stating they were Muslim. Behiç discussed this idea with the Turkish Imam of the Paris mosque, and asked him if he would be willing to furnish the Turkish Jews (if they asked) with a document declaring them to be Muslim. Affirming that saving lives was a holy deed, the Imam agreed and began issuing the documents whenever they were requested.

* * *

Slowly but surely, the Germans were making their way towards Vichy. That November, forty-six year old Lt. General Hans Roland Krug von Nidda became the German delegate to Vichy, with the title of Consul-General. On December 1, 1941, a meeting between Field Marshal Pétain and Field Marshal Göring was held at Saint-Florentin, Vergigny. The following statement regarding this meeting was released by Benois Mechin, the French Minister of State: "Subsequent to the meetings between Pétain and Hitler at Montore on October 25,1940 and Hitler and Darlan on May 11 1941, this meeting between the two Field Marshals marks a new era in French-German cooperation."

Behiç could not immediately grasp the real agenda behind the meeting and he was very curious.

Consul-General Krug von Nidda, known as a temperamental man, requested a meeting with Behic at the Turkish Embassy on December 9. When von Nidda arrived, panic broke out among the hundreds of Jews waiting at the embassy gates. Von Nidda was also shocked to see so many Jews milling around in front of and inside the Turkish Embassy. Since the Ambassador had no idea why von Nidda wanted to see him, he was cautious and welcomed him to the embassy, commenting that the visit must be standard procedure for von Nidda.

"I have no intention of visiting all the embassies. I specifically came here to see you. My dear Ambassador, I know of you from our commanders stationed in Anatolia during the Ottoman period. After I was appointed here and learned you were the Turkish Ambassador, I was very happy that I would have the opportunity to meet you in person."

Maintaining his diplomatic demeanor and unsure of what von Nidda had been told, Behic explained that he worked with German officers for several years and felt that everyone learned a lot. While there were many instances of both agreement and disagreement, the relationship was always one of mutual respect whereupon Krug von Nidda laughed out loud.

"I wouldn't be surprised if there were no instances of agreement. No officer, especially one who is a member of an army that has deep-rooted traditions reaching back hundreds of years like the Ottomans, would have been content with the appointment of foreign officers as commanders. However, from what I had heard, you managed to upset General von Schellendorf (Chairman of the Joint Chiefs of Staff).

Behic didn't want to be drawn in to any superficial debate at that moment so he invited von Nidda to dine with him after the New Year and discuss their ideas. Agreeing, von Nidda suggested that the dinner be at his headquarters with the Ambassador as guest. The date set, secretary Zeki accompanied the von Nidda to the door of the embassy. As soon as their guest had left, Zeki rushed back to Behiç's office to tell him about the scene he had just witnessed. Von Nidda was so disgusted at seeing all the Jews, he walked quite gingerly down the stairs avoiding any contact with anyone as if they all had leprosy and he might get the disease if he came too close.

"I cannot fathom how you were able to work with them for all those years."

"Life is full of surprises and you have to keep your cool while constantly planning two or three moves ahead as though you are playing a game of chess. In lieu of using a real gun, diplomacy is your strongest weapon. Diplomacy requires patience and intelligence and apparently I was fairly good at diplomacy since the Germans always complained about me but still awarded me their highest medals. That, my friend, is what diplomacy is all about. Join me at this dinner and you'll have a better understanding."

My grandfather and Sedat Zeki had dinner with Consul-General Krug von Nidda on the evening of January 24, 1942 as planned. Von Nidda could barely contain himself and admitted his eagerness to hear the Ambassador's experiences with German officers during WWI. As Behic explained, the thought among the generals at the time was that the German method of military organization would be the best model to follow. When the Germans sailed their battleships *Goben* and *Breslau* through the Dardanelles Straits, the Ottoman government purchased the ships, changing their names to *Yavuz* and *Midilli,*and made Admiral Suchon a Turkish commander instead of remaining neutral which would have allowed them to disarm those vessels. When the newly created Turkish commander Suchon entered the Black Sea to lob shells at Russian ports on November 1, 1914, the Turks found themselves legally in the fray on the side of the Germans.

As a result, Turkish officers worked directly or indirectly with German officers. In Behic's case he worked with Field Marshal Liman von Sanders, Chairman of the Ottoman Joint Chiefs of Staff General Bronsart von Schellendorf, Field Marshal von der Goltz, General Kannengeisser and Major Baare. Rather than regale von Nidda with war stories, The Ambassador recounted incidents that he felt would have a subtle influence on his host.

"Let me tell you what transpired between me and General Bronsart von Schellendorf. I think you'll find it interesting. In December of 1916, von Schellendorf summoned me quite late at night and when I saw that General Enver, the War Minister of the Ottoman Joint Chiefs of Staff, was there I assumed it was something quite serious. As I approached Enver he beckoned me into his office and called in his Aide De Camp. Enver seemed quite upset and he told me that there was a communications problem. He didn't know German and von Schellendorf didn't know Turkish. They both spoke French but the German General refused to speak the language of the enemy, therefore since Behic spoke German, he had to deal with the General.

von Schellendorf: "Issue the order to the army that from now on it will use the Gregorian calendar." The Ottomans used the Islamic calendar called Rumi calendar at the time. Behic: "I'm going to need some explanations from the General."

von Schellendorf: "I beg your pardon, Colonel, aren't you aware that issued orders need to be executed immediately?'"

Behic: "I'm well aware of that; but leave our army out of it. First of all, we are not on the battlefront; secondly, I'm a duty yeoman assigned to the Ministry of War; I'm not a member of the headquarters staff. If the General doesn't provide answers to my questions, it won't be possible to issue his order."

Impatient and put out, von Schellendorf said: "Fire away."

Behic: "What year is it going to be? What date will the year start with? If I don't give the army this information, the Army Office will be asked the questions but won't have the answers. The General knows that it is easier to issue orders than to carry them out; they can be applied, but I want to issue a definite order."

von Schellendorf: "I don't need lessons from a Colonel. I know the questions asked. Go see General Enver tomorrow."

"Following directions, I went to see Enver who told me to issue the order that the year would be 1916 and begin with the month of January.

Since the order, as it stood, only applied to the army, Enver suggested that we state that the Ministry of Finance was preparing the law and once ratified by the Assembly, the calendar would be valid for the general public. I responded that it was his edict, but if the calendar project was amended in the Parliament Assembly, that meant we would have to change the order. I suggested we just wait until it became a law. Enver agreed and told me to pressure the Ministry of Finance to have the law passed over to the Assembly as soon as possible.

That afternoon, I called on the Minister of Finance and explained the situation, The Assembly ratified the law with a date difference of 13 days and no changes regarding the year (1916) with a starting date of January 1. General von Schellendorf was furious with me, believing that I was responsible for the modifications. He complained to a German Army delegation, describing me as a conservative. After that we never had a moment's peace with General von Schellendorf. But I did have another run-in with him.

On August 3, 1917, Field Marshal von Sanders' Deputy Staff Officer Kâzım (later General Kâzım □nanç), presented me with a 2nd Degree Iron Cross Order on behalf of von Sanders. When I asked why I was receiving such an honor, Colonel Kâzım explained that von Sanders was impressed with the way the logistics were handled in the Gallipoli campaign and wanted to know who was in charge of the operation. Field Marshal von Sanders proposed to the German Emperor that I receive this order."

Von Nidda had been attentive while Behic spoke but interrupted him at this point in the story.

"So you have an Iron Cross, Mr. Ambassador?"

"Yes."

Von Nidda's expression changed slightly. Rarely were foreigners presented with the Iron Cross.

Behiç continued. "One day, I was walking down the stairs at the War Ministry, about to go to Friday prayers. I was wearing the Iron Cross with my other medals when I met General von Schellendorf on the landing and greeted him respectfully. He stopped and asked in a cold, derisive demeanor when had I received this medal, pointing at the Iron Cross, and who presented it to me? I looked him straight in the eye and told him that the German Emperor presented it to me.

Quite stiffly he countered with "You do know that this is a great honor?" and then turned and walked away.

Sometime later I told Enver about the exchange and he informed me that von Schellendorf became quite depressed about it because even though he held the title of Chairman of the Ottoman Army's Joint Chiefs of Staff and the rank of General in the German Army, the highest medal he had been awarded was the same 2nd Degree Iron Cross that I had. Perhaps he felt he deserved more recognition but he blew the whole situation out of proportion. Needless to say, the relationship between Field Marshal von Sanders and General von Schellendorf steadily worsened to the point that the latter was recalled to Germany."

At that point von Nidda remarked that the General was right because not everyone was privileged to receive such a medal. Rising from his chair, von Nidda lifted his goblet and toasted the Iron Cross.

"Even General Kannengeisser went to the extent of asking my opinion about every order that originated from general headquarters. Actually, that worked out well because I was able to have many decisions changed which would have been impossible to apply to our Ottoman army. General Kannengeisser didn't believe me when I told him that General Enver considered everything the Germans had to say as more correct so I suggested he test my theory by presenting one of my ideas to Enver as his and one of his ideas as if it was mine. When Enver accepted the idea he thought was Kannengeisser's and rejected the idea he thought was mine, he realized I was right.

There was one particular conversation we had that I have never forgotten. I still hurt every time I look at a map and remember it. One day I read in the papers that the German Empire proposed a ceasefire under the condition that the status quo was preserved. When I arrived at the office, I mentioned this news to General Kannengeisser who said he had heard all about it. I asked him if this was the case, what would become of our Eastern provinces and our occupied territories in Iraq? I expected him to say something about Germany standing by her allies but his reply shocked and grieved me. He told me that 'Those areas are of no concern to us. If you've got it in you, then you can go and reclaim all that territory.' As you can imagine I was speechless. The reason why places like Mosul and Kirkuk are today included on a map of Iraq is because of this ceasefire."

Now von Nidda was speechless. A minute ago he was full of enthusiasm, enchanted by the stories of his country pinning medals of distinction on Behiç's chest. Suddenly the bubble burst as Behiç blamed the loss of Turkish territory like Mosul and Kirkuk on German indifference. The silence didn't last as von Nidda switched gears and asked my grandfather if it was true that he, meaning the Turkish embassy and Consulates, was helping Jews.

"We are not doing anything else but carrying out our duty within the framework of my nation's laws and regulations regarding the rights of our Jewish citizens who arrived here years ago to work temporarily."

"Your Embassy is filled to the rafters with Jews," objected von Nidda. "I saw that with my own eyes."

"Let me assure you, Mr. Consul-General," Behiç asserted. "No one from the public is allowed to enter my embassy unless they are Turkish citizens." In his memoirs, Grandfather wrote that he paused to let those words sink in. "I hope I can count on you to assist me whenever I contact you to discuss problems that are encountered regarding my citizens?" Grandpa wrote that von Nidda remained silent but his face turned red.

On the way back to the embassy, Sedat Zeki said he was fascinated by the evening and appreciated how diplomacy could be used to tie someone up in a ball and toss him in a corner!

"When the German Consul-General heard you were awarded the 2nd Degree Iron Cross, he looked as though he was going to stand up and salute you!"

"Then he probably would have stumbled over backwards if I had told him I was awarded the 1st Degree Iron Cross as well!"

"You have one of those, too?!" Sedat Zeki exclaimed.

"Field Marshal von Sanders personally awarded me the 1st Degree medal, saying 'This is my country's order of the highest degree,' as he pinned it on my chest. You know, I've always wondered what General von Schellendorf's reaction might have been if he learned I received the 1st Degree Iron Cross also."

NEWSPAPERS AND THE NEW LAWS

* * *

Behiç was greatly annoyed that the newspapers printed in Paris were unavailable in the Unoccupied Zone so he
requested that the French Ministry of Foreign Affairs make
them available. When his request was ignored he decided
to bring up the subject during one of his customary weekly
meetings with the Foreign Minister's Undersecretary. As
Turkey's Ambassador to France he had the right to know
what was happening in the country and he assured the
undersecretary that the newspapers would remain in the
embassy. When the papers arrived, Behic was distressed
by the blatant anti-Semitic content not to mention the
anti-Allied powers and anti-Vichy rhetoric.

When it came to the lives of his Turkish Jews, Behiç
was determined to keep up the pressure on the French
authorities concerning their discriminatory behavior and
continued to submit official objections to oppressive laws
imposed upon Jewish Turks.

He wrote a letter to the Vichy government in August of
1941 reiterating his ideas. "I verbally stated to you that the
Turkish government will not remain indifferent to the conditions imposed on its Jewish citizens in France. Once again, I
would like to remind you of the doctrines and stance taken
by the Turkish government regarding this issue. Though we
do not have any objection regarding the point of foreigners complying with the laws of their host countries, we
don't condone the practice of discrimination against
Turkish citizens who have settled abroad. In this context,
by means of Diplomatic Note No. 912/6127, dated 31 July

1941, the Turkish Embassy has informed its citizens that it shall protect all their rights and privileges."

As Behiç negotiated with top-level officials regarding his objections to the new laws and tried to come up with solutions regarding the problems of Turkish citizens by telephoning, writing communiqués, or paying personal visits to lower level French officials, the Germans were implementing their sanctions against Jewish businesses and property in the occupied territory as quickly as possible. A great deal of the embassy's communications were conducted via police chiefs, local governors, occupying German officers, including army commanders, SS officers, Gestapo and concentration camp commanders. In order to establish contact with individuals sent to a concentration camp, their citizenship details had to be transmitted to the relevant Consulate, and then sent to the German Ambassador in Paris, Otto Abetz, who then relayed this information to the relevant concentration camp commander.

Abetz was probably the last person in France one would want to encounter when dealing with the affairs of the Jews because he was Adolf Eichmann's representative. Unfortunately it was necessary to officially file requests with Abetz to release Turkish citizens from detention.

VICHY 1942

* * *

Field Marshal Pétain entertained the entire diplomatic corps on New Year's Day, 1942, at a luncheon given at The Park Hotel. The Japanese attack on Pearl Harbor December 7 brought America into the war on the side of the allies while Japan was part of the Axis coalition. The change of events affected diplomatic protocol and made seating arrangements tricky.

The protocol for seating arrangements had always been based on the tenure of the ambassadors, which put Japan and America next to each other. The Chief of Protocol, Baron de Bauverger, was having a difficult time trying to remedy the situation. By the time Marshal Pétain arrived in the dining room the problem still had not been solved so there was nothing left to do but arrange the seating as they always had which meant that France was seated next to Brazil, then Argentina, Spain, Turkey, America and Japan.

All eyes were on the American and Japanese Ambassadors as Pétain greeted everyone with a few words and a cordial handshake. Approaching the American Ambassador he asked the group rhetorically if they were all going to eat together making sure that the message was not lost on either the American or the Japanese. During a private moment with Behic a week later Petain asked if he was worried about the Nazis who had advance to the Bulgarian border, quite close to Turkey. When Behic responded with a forceful "no", Petain confided in him,

"They give promises they can't keep; they tell lies; they'll go behind your back. So just be careful."

In keeping with the directives issued by Vichy concerning the appointment of directors to operate the businesses that the Jewish owners were forced to relinquish, Behiç sent Communiqué No. 96-6127 to the Marseilles Consulate-General in January of 1942. Reading the communiqué that my grandfather had copied into his memoirs as well as the accompanying notes, it was obvious that Behiç tried so diligently to follow the day-to-day goings on. It seemed that he was more than an ambassador. He was a caring relative trying to do whatever he could to help and protect his family. This document emphasized the sensitivity Behiç showed when dealing with the myriad problems facing the Jews.

To Marseilles he wrote, "I came up with a formula to combat the Vichy government's innate stubbornness, and even sent a diplomatic note to them regarding this issue. You need to handle the pertinent preparations immediately, without wasting any time. In fact, go and remind the Jewish Task Force that when we previously warned them, they promised us they would act with sensitivity on issues concerning us. Also, have them cease all measures imposed against my citizens. Don't forget to keep me updated on this subject on a daily basis; in fact, have the Consulate-General staff conduct research and let me know if they come up with anything we can use in our favor."

Behic wanted Turkish Jewish businesses to be turned over to Turkish Muslim directors but not just any Turks. These people had to have been living in France for the past 10 years without any sort of criminal record, who lived at the same address for the past five years, who had been working at the same job for the past three years, and who were married with children. When people with those requirements were located, they were invited to meet with Behic who presented his ideas to them.

"These days, our Turkish Jews are faced with the distinct possibility of losing everything they have acquired through years of hard work. There is no racial, religious or language discrimination in our country. These types of discriminating and acrimonious measures are not a part of our religion, our history, our customs, or our traditions. As the Turkish Ambassador, I wish to emphasize that as long as I remain here at this post, I consider myself entrusted with the lives and property of all our Turkish citizens, regardless of religion or race. I have given instructions to have my staff do whatever is necessary to protect the lives of our citizens.

However, we are faced with an unforeseeable situation. Even as I speak, the assets, property, businesses, and everything that the Turkish Jews have accumulated are in danger. In this situation, we are going to voice our objections with all the appropriate authorities. However, I believe that we need to take all the necessary precautions to counter worse case scenarios. In this context, according to my criteria, you are trustworthy Turkish citizens. You all have children and lead stable lives. It is for these very reasons that I'm going to ask something of you that might bear some very heavy responsibilities.

You are not obliged to accept this duty. This is a weight that not everyone would be able to handle easily; this is a matter of honor, one that requires resolve, one that requires responsibility, one that requires humanity. We are a nation that has succeeded in pulling together as a single entity in every war of our recent past. The property of our Jewish citizens will be transferred over to those of you who temporarily accept responsibility under legal oath until the conclusion of the war. Those who accept the task will be the ones providing the guarantee. However, we are going to present the list of those who accept this task to the Jewish community. They are the ones who are going to decide, not the Embassy or the Consulates. The core of this idea is to present this as a list of our self-sacrificing Turkish citizens who meet the criteria of taking on this responsibility and who have volunteered to extend a helping hand in these ominous times. The Jewish citizens are going to decide for themselves because this responsibility is great.

Most of those who attended the meeting became signatories of a document titled "Turkish guarantors who have been appointed enterprises belonging to dispersed Jewish Turks."

Behiç immediately informed Ankara about his solution in Communiqué No.228/162/6127 despite the fact that Vichy would not accept the idea of appointing Turks instead of temporary French administrators to operate the businesses of the Turkish Jews. However, he did manage to pull an "end run" by convincing the Jewish Task Force, which was under greater German influence, his idea was good. This particular Communiqué demonstrated that the French were determined to be more German than the Germans with the "we are just following orders attitude" and that Behic knew how to circumvent Vichy and work with the Germans .

Though his plan had merit there just weren't enough candidates who met Behiç's criteria for custodial responsibility and while more than half of the Turkish citizens living in France resided in and around Paris, the number of those who met his criteria lived in and around the city of Vichy. How to solve the problem? Have one custodian look after more than one business. My grandfather reproduced the report to Ankara in his memoirs.

I had previously reported details concerning the regime which applies to the Jews here. This situation affects our citizens of the Jewish race who live in the Unoccupied Zone and I would like to inform you of their current position:

1-   As for the practices implemented on our Jewish citizens that I previously reported toyou, this has been confirmed in the form of a diplomatic note to the French Ministry of Foreign Affairs stating that we would reserve all our rights vis-à-vis all such practices. Though we have yet to receive a written reply to this memo, the General Secretary of the department dealing with our country's affairs, M. Outrey, indicated on another occasion that it would be impossible to acquiesce to our demand. Naturally, we responded by saying that our government was right and that it wasn't going to alter its stance. During this conversation, M. Outrey stated that the Germans coerced the French to implement the anti-Jewish practices and hinted objectively that the French Government's decision to continue applying these practices along with their ultimate form will follow the general chain of global events. It is clear the French Ministry of Foreign Affairs continues to maintain the same stance with other foreign diplomats who have brought up the same issue.

2-   As of last month, Jewish foreign nationals living in the Unoccupied Zone, including those of Turkish nationality, have been assigned 'custodians' to take over their business operations.

Regarding the application of these rules, the French Government has insisted that no distinction will be made between the nationalities of the Jewish population on French soil and that our efforts to prevent custodians from being assigned to businesses owned by Jewish Turks will be to no avail. Consequently, this dilemma has been solved by assigning Turkish administrators to businesses owned by Jewish Turks. In light of the timidity shown by the French Ministry of Foreign Affairs to become involved in this matter, a positive result was assured through our direct contacts at the Jewish Task Force.

A list of managerial candidates has been compiled by the Embassy and will be conveyed to the Jewish Task Force, which will make a selection from this list.

However, a serious problem cropped up while compiling this list; the number of non-Jewish Turkish citizens residing in Unoccupied France who are able to carry out the business of "temporary management" honestly and in a serious fashion was determined to be quite low.

In carrying out our efforts regarding the matter of custodians, both the French Ministry of Foreign Affairs and the Jewish Task Force were informed that we are upholding the rights of our citizens to counter the practices taken against Jews and that they were requested not to block our efforts of ascertaining a viable solution to this matter based on our principles. As the application of the solution regarding the aforementioned matter of the custodians is about to be implemented, I am currently not in the position to provide you with any sort of applicable results.

3-   However, I want to underline the point that despite the fact that we have come up with a solution to the matter of the custodians, it does not constitute a guarantee against possible harm and damages that may befall our Jewish citizens in the future.

In reality, in reviewing the French legislation regarding this matter, it is understood that minimum subsistence payments rendered from the revenue earned from operations and product sales will be made by the custodians to the owners whose operations and property they were entrusted with. The remainder of the earned funds must be turned over to the French Government. As a final point, even though the opportunity does exist for Jewish owners and custodians to parlay the sum to be paid to the French Government to an absolute minimum, this will not always be the case, making one wonder what is to become of all that Jewish money that will soon be flowing into the French Government's coffers. It is a very strong possibility that sooner or later, the French Government is going to appropriate these funds.

With my esteemed regards,

The Turkish Ambassador to Paris
Behiç Erkin

In March, the Marseilles Consulate presented the embassy with a stumbling block. The Jewish Task Force in Nice would not accept the appointment of Turkish Muslim custodians to oversee the businesses of Turkish Jews but they observe the French custodians who would be assigned.

When Brazilian Ambassador Souza-Dantas paid one of his regular visits to the Turkish Embassy, he asked my grandfather what he was doing to counter the decisions taken by the French government regarding Turkey's Jewish citizens because he, too, wanted to save helpless victims from the Germans. Behic showed Souza-Dantas the communiqué about the task force telling him, 'Look…this is not child's play we're talking about here; check out this statement. Yes today, No tomorrow. The following day, maybe. What audacity! The Jewish Task Force in Vichy says one thing; the Jewish Task Force in Nice says something entirely different. I'm involved in a diplomatic battle on four separate fronts. One, with the French in the Occupied Zone; two, with the Germans; three, with the French in the Unoccupied Zone; and four, with the Jewish Task Force. From whichever one I get the desired result, I immediately give instructions for implementation. But as you see, neither the French nor the Germans stick to their word. Nobody's expecting them to but I would be happy if they were able to stick to their word for at least a few months!" Moving a little closer to the Brazilian as though someone might be listening, the ambassador said:

"Do you know what my real problem is, Souza-Dantas? It's my genes, the mannerisms I got from my ancestors, as well as my country's religion, customs and traditions. They turned me into a conscientious, responsible person so I lose a lot of sleep dealing with the injustice and unfairness that our helpless Jewish citizens face. On the other hand, I'm doing a little conscience bookkeeping with the Almighty on the presumption he will forgive me in case I don't succeed completely. I keep running this question through my mind. Why are the Christians plundering the goods, property, and lives of the Jews, while Allah's Muslim servants, my embassy and consulate staffs, are trying to salvage the situation? I'm sure God is enjoying the irony of all this!"

The Brazilian Ambassador was taken by surprise because what Grandpa said was the truth. It was the Christians who were burning and destroying the Jews while the Muslims were trying to save the Jews.

"It is necessary to carry out one's duties. It is we who have the responsibility, and it is we, the ambassadors, who have been entrusted with the lives and possessions of our citizens who live here in a foreign country. With regards to these events, I believe the Germans and French are committing mistakes on a monstrous scale. I'm going to try to do everything I can and I humbly suggest that you do the same. What's more, I'm going to suggest to my government that whatever the French subject our citizens to here should be applied tit-for-tat in our country!"

RETALIATION

* * *

Regarding the Turkish Embassy communiqué dated January 22, 1942, in which the businesses of Turkish citizens Mr. Ali Arslan and Mr. David Kohen are to be assigned custodians by the Jewish Task Force, this situation has been brought to the attention of our Ministry of Foreign Affairs. The Turkish Embassy has requested that administrators to be appointed to Jewish business be chosen from amongst Turkish citizens. In response to this request, our Ministry of Foreign Affairs wishes to inform the Turkish Embassy that the Jewish Task Force does not accept the idea of appointing administrators of the same nationality as foreign national Jews.

On the other hand, in order to provide the Turkish Embassy with a satisfactory answer and in order for the Turkish Embassy to take the best interests of its own citizens into consideration, we are willing to accept having the Embassy nominate Turkish citizens as observers next to the French administrators.

In this context, the Ministry of Foreign Affairs will be pleased to confirm to the Turkish Embassy that Mr. Muhtar and Mr. Kandemir shall be able to conduct what is expected from them as 'observers' alongside the administrators of the properties of Mr. Ali Arslan and Mr. David Kohen.

After reading this letter, Behic burst out "Who the hell do they think they're fooling? They're walking on pins and needles over there so as not to disappoint us. They've made it seem as though the Jewish Task Force rejected us, but that they, the Ministry of Foreign Affairs, came up with a solution. They've invented this stupid, ineffective, incapable observer status formula?!"

Behic then deciphered the letter for a confused Sedat Zeki. "Mr. Turkish Ambassador, you want us, the French Government, to appoint Turkish administrators for these two Jews? Well, even if we were an official organization, we don't have any say over the Jewish Task Force. We've decided to use the German's pig-headed behavior against the Jews to our own benefit, and in order to appear charming in their eyes, we established an institution called the Jewish Task Force. Then we made France's biggest enemy of the Jews, Xavier Vallat, the head of that institution so the Germans don't get too wound up. Even though officially this institution is French, spiritually and unofficially speaking, it's a German institution. And though we put in a request for you, we couldn't get them to accept it; so we found a formula that won't prevent them from their ultimate goal of commandeering the Jews' property, money, their homes, and everything else. So please, just put up with it."

Leon Mandil who worked in the embassy overheard Behic, suddenly turned white and crumbled up in his chair. Sedat Zeki loosened his tie while Behiç grabbed the bottle of lemon-scented cologne he kept in his drawer. The cologne revived Mandil who apologized explaining that he was Jewish with a family and the whole situation suddenly hit him like the proverbial ton of bricks and for a moment, he couldn't breathe.

"Mr. Mandil, we are going to have to fight harder against these slovenly pigs, so there's no passing out while we've still got a long way to go. We can't lose because we have to give hope and strength to our helpless citizens. There are many women and children downstairs who should definitely not see you in this state, so I'm asking you to pull yourself together. Let me assure you that this Turkish gentleman won't be discouraged by the French who play the butler role to the Germans. But in return, I'm asking you to maintain your composure in the Embassy, on the street and even with your family. We might have received an extremely unpleasant outcome today, but that won't prevent tomorrow from coming. Of course we'll come up with a solution for this situation. Just keep in mind that what you hear at the Embassy stays at the Embassy.

The French couldn't bring us down with cannons and rifles, so there's no way they're going to beat us down with diplomacy. We know how to look after our people despite their counter-assaults. I compare this situation we are in, which has manifested itself in the form of continual opposing assault, with a situation Mustafa Kemal wrote me about in 1912. The Italians threw everything they had, eight, nine times at the lines Mustafa Kemal set up but they couldn't breach them. I believe it was nine times! So, don't worry, we are not about to crumple in the face of two or three French attacks."

Near Behic's desk was a chest he had brought with him from Budapest. In fact, when the embassy moved from Paris to Vichy, Behiç personally took charge of moving the chest. No one knew what was in the chest but everyone at the embassy was curious about it and there was always some speculation about what it contained. Only once was Behic asked what was in the chest and his response had been, "History." No one ever asked again. Sedat Zeki and Leon Mandil watched in surprise as Behiç began fiddling with the lock. The chest may have contained history but for them, this was an historic moment. Behic pulled the letter from Ataturk that he had just mentioned and put it on his desk. Both men were in awe and stood looking at it. The letter seemed to bring them both joy and sadness and they were able to release the tension of the previous moments.

"Come on, let's get back to work. Forget about the chest and whether it was locked up or not, don't you have anything better to do?"

Both men left the room, feeling better whereas only 10 minutes had passed since they were depressed about their work. Behiç had succeeded once more in getting his staff back into a positive frame of mind.

Demonstrating his constant decisiveness, Behiç voiced his objections to the communiqué from the Ministry of Foreign Affairs by replying that the Turkish Embassy still had every intention of defending the rights of its Jewish citizens to the very end:

This attitude of the Jewish Task Force surprises the Turkish Embassy since Monsieur René Gazagne, Director of the Statut du Personnel at the aforementioned Jewish Task Force, declared to the First Secretary of our embassy in the course of a conversation on this subject that provisional Turkish administrators would be appointed for Turkish Jews and on the basis of this agreement in principle our embassy has already sent to the Jewish Task Force our list of candidates. The nomination of provisional Turkish administrators for the properties of Turkish Jews, which our embassy had requested, while maintaining our government's reservation on the entire question of applying to its citizens the French laws and regulations regarding Jews, constitutes in our eyes the most normal possible solution to the exceptional situation in question (by the fact that it restores the administration of the interests of Turks of Jewish race into the hands of persons of the same nationality) and the best measure to assure the minimum guarantee in favor of the parties, while awaiting a definitive solution conforming to international rules and customs.

Turkish Ambassador,
Behiç Erkin

LAVAL IN VICHY

* * *

At the beginning of April Behic learned via a journalist that the word on Embassy Row was that Pierre Laval was going to assume the reins of power in Vichy. Apparently the Germans were unhappy with the way Vichy was being administered. German Undersecretary Achenbach went to Vichy from Paris, met with Madame Petain, and told her that France was not following policies with Germany's best interests in mind and warned her that Vichy could expect a fate similar to that of Belgrade, in other words, a barrage of aerial bombings. Frightened, Madame Petain related the details of the meeting to her husband. In the meantime Abetz, the German Ambassador, told Laval that the groundwork had been prepared for Laval to go to Vichy and confront the Field Marshal. Abetz reminded Laval that he had been rescued from disaster by the Germans in 1940 and it was now payback time.

The next day the Vichy newspapers carried the story that because the foreign policy of France was in grave danger, Laval carried out his civic duty by explaining this to the Field Marshal. A few days later, Laval assumed control of the government, both the Interior and Foreign Ministries, and made changes in the cabinet.

My grandfather wrote about an experience with Laval that gave me goose bumps when I first read it. Laval visited the Turkish embassy and after several minutes of mindless chatter finally came to the reason for his visit. The Germans wanted "workers" and he had just come from a visit with the Spanish ambassador who said he didn't think his government would prevent Spanish refugees in France from being sent to Germany. Laval then asked my grandfather if the Turkish embassy would also send workers to which the reply was a resounding no. As Laval was leaving the embassy he asked Behic who he thought should be Laval's ambassador to Ankara. Needless to say Grandpa was taken aback by the question so he said nothing. When Laval asked him again, Behic explained that he had no opinion. He was merely the ambassador of the Turkish government. After Laval left Behic turned to Sedat Zeki and shaking his head in amazement told Zeki that the President of the Vichy government is knocking on all the embassy doors in an effort to find workers for the Germans. "Can you believe that, Sedat Zeki, can you believe it? If I hadn't heard it with my own ears I wouldn't believe it myself. May God bring all of this to a favorable conclusion, because by the look of things, this is going to be a long, hard, journey!"

As protocol demanded, Laval's visit had to be reciprocated and Behiç wanted to touch on a few issues regarding the Turkish Jews, but he didn't know how to approach the subject with such an obvious German sympathizer. Obviously he couldn't just blurt out what he wanted to say; the conversation had to develop. During the course of their talk Laval made the statement that it was President Roosevelt who was responsible for Laval's political rise. When Roosevelt heard the rumor that Laval was going to head the government he informed Pétain through the U.S. Ambassador Admiral Leahy it would be considered an unfriendly gesture. When Hitler heard this he supposedly declared that although it was his army that occupied France, he doesn't get mixed up in the country's domestic affairs. But if Roosevelt wanted to stick his two pfennigs in, then Hitler would as well and Laval was reinstated.

Behiç was at a point in his ongoing diplomatic fight with the French and Germans where he felt his government had to use its diplomatic powers and he said as much in a critical communiqué, No. 597/383, written on May 15,1942. Behiç Erkin had been a commander in the War of Liberation in which he fought against the Greeks, against those who accepted English servitude and those who accepted the American mandate as well as the government in Istanbul. His belief was that the reason Ankara won that war was because Ataturk had faith in the people. What Behiç Erkin wanted from Ankara was that when the time came they have the same faith in him.

A couple of days later, Behic asked Sedat Zeki and Leon Mandil to find a lawyer who specialized in international law and a good historian. The men looked at each other quizzically but neither asked the ambassador why he wanted these particular people brought to the embassy. For several days, Behic, the lawyer, and the historian worked together privately.

This is a supplement to Communiqué No. 228/162/6127, dated February 16, 1942. In that communiqué, I wrote that although we had reached a favorable outcome in discussions with the General Jewish Task Force regarding the necessity of appointing Turkish citizens as custodians of businesses owned by our Jewish citizens in the Unoccupied Zone, I mentioned that I wasn't able to provide any information regarding this agreement because it hadn't been put into writing yet.

Unfortunately, ensuing events have shown my doubts to be correct: Despite the fact that we had previously come to a verbal agreement on this matter with the Jewish Task Force, the diplomatic note we subsequently received from the French Ministry of Foreign Affairs stated that they didn't find it suitable for said Task Force to appoint temporary Turkish administrators but that they were prepared to accept Turkish observers alongside the French administrators to be appointed to handle the business of our Jewish citizens.

This unusual proposal regarding Turkish observers would not be sufficient even to assure the desired minimum outcome. In fact, in dealing with administrative affairs of said businesses, these observers would have no right to interfere, but would only be able to inform Turkish authorities whenever they came across instances of impropriety. Observers would be incapable of handling even this task since the extent of any damage or corruption caused by the French administrators would be unknown and therefore impossible to repair once Turkish observers blow the whistle.

In view of this situation, the response by the French Ministry of Foreign Affairs to our request constitutes the minimum solution for us. Actually, despite the verbal agreement regarding our request to the Jewish Task Force, we regret that this decision has been reversed. While in declaring that we continue to affirm the rights that we announced in regards to our Jewish citizens, we have provided a response to the extent of insisting that our demands regarding the matter of "observer" status to be examined once more.

Although we presented this in written form, we still have not received a response to our diplomatic note. Meanwhile, we are learning that French administrators are continuing to be appointed as directors of the businesses of our Jewish citizens. I am presenting you with a list of those who have been subjected to this conduct up until now. Previously, embassies that took the same tack are now encountering the same treatment. Because the situation has dragged on interminably, our Jewish citizens are suffering damages.

For this reason, I believe that the time has come to take the diplomatic initiative by exerting pressure on the French Ministry of Foreign Affairs. In light of this situation, I *think that it would be appropriate for us to retaliate against the French. This retaliation, in whatever shape or form it takes, should highlight our country's principles regarding our non-discriminatory religious, racial and language policies. It would be most appropriate for this action to be taken not only against French Jews, but rather against all French citizens residing in Turkey.*

The Paris Ambassador
Behiç Erkin

This communiqué sent shockwaves throughout Ankara. Adding to President İnönü's concerns was the attitude of Foreign Minister Numan Menemencioğlu who wondered why the president thought Behiç Erkin was the best man for the job. Perhaps if he understood the situation in Vichy he wouldn't have had any doubts. The Ambassador used personal relations as well as official channels when he wanted a favorable outcome on the subject of his Jewish citizens. To that extent he had invited Vichy President Pierre Laval to luncheon with him the following day.

Sedat Zeki remembered this incident well and related the story to me. Zeki was nervous because so much was at stake and he asked Behic if the topic of the Turkish Jews was going to be discussed. With a devious look on his face Grandpa Behic replied that they would be 'conducting diplomacy'. Assuming that Behic was going to do to Laval what he did with von Nidda, he became excited but Behic was quick to calm him down.

"Diplomacy, Sedat Zeki, is like a sharp, double-edged knife. We need to be careful here. It needs proper planning, choosing the right time, and not allowing the other party to gain the upper hand. Otherwise, that knife will turn and cut you. I'll tell you this much; I've been planning this in my head for days now.

Please bring me a copy of the communiqué I sent to Ankara yesterday and those bottles of wine I brought from Budapest. It's very important that the atmosphere is relaxed and congenial; it should be jubilant! That's why I've invited Brazilian ambassador Souza-Dantas to ensure that's what happens!"

"Do you think President Laval will be bothered when he sees the Jews coming to the embassy on official business?" asked Zeki.

"Have we been sending out all those letters for nothing?" replied Behiç. "I hope the embassy will be more crowded than it normally is,"

Because President Laval went home every evening to his home 15 kilometers from Vichy in the village of Chateldon, he insisted on afternoon events.

Laval arrived with Foreign Affairs Undersecretary Rochat, M. Lagarde, also of the Ministry of Foreign Affairs, Chief of Protocol Baron Bouverger and State Minister Admiral Platon.

It would have been impossible for the French delegation to miss all the Jews gathered in front of the gate and overflowing throughout the embassy premises. Sedat Zeki received greeted them ushered them into the dining room where Ambassador Behiç offered his guests glasses of the famous Hungarian Tokay wine. Tasting this wine for the first time, Laval was impressed and commented that now he understood why Tokay was served in all the palaces.

The luncheon went well. The more Laval drank, the more he talked; the more he talked, the more he drank. At one point during the meal, Laval told of his meeting with Stalin. After visiting Rome and the Vatican, Laval went to Moscow and told Stalin that the Pope was grieved by all the religious persecution going on in Russia. Everyone at the table was attentive, listening to the story.

"Stalin asked me, 'How many soldiers can the Pope mobilize?' "I said to Stalin, 'As you know, the Pope's power is spiritual.' "Stalin replied, 'then the Pope's words don't interest me in the least.'" Then, Laval began to tell about meeting Hitler. Sedat Zeki said he began to wonder if Behic was ever going to be able to talk to Laval about what was really important.

According to Laval, "One day, Ambassador Abetz told me I was going to meet with a great German statesman. Abetz didn't know who he was or where he was staying but the same day they sent me on my way." The Germans had Laval going from vehicle to vehicle with various officials until he ended up at Montoire, where Hitler was residing. It was then that he realized he was going to meet Der Fuehrer.

When the luncheon ended and the French delegation rose to leave, Behiç asked Laval to accompany him to his office. On the way he asked Laval if Sedat Zeki could join them since his French was excellent. On the wall in the office was a painting of an Ottoman General.

Drawing Laval's attention to that painting, Behic explained that he had always been interested in history and since his appointment as ambassador to France, began studying relations between countries. In particular, Behic looked at the history of the relationship between Turkey and France which dated back to the 15th century, a fact that he found fascinating.

"I wonder how many other countries have managed to remain friends with France on the diplomatic front for almost 500 years?" asked Behiç.

"I don't know," replied Laval, "five at the most. But I suppose you forgot about the battle that Napoleon Bonaparte fought against the Ottomans on the outskirts of Acre in Palestine.

Sedat Zeki said that he felt his stomach flip at that point.

"Your Excellency," Behiç said, "history is rife with emperors who weren't able to bridle their ambitions. That wouldn't harm the past and future relations between the people of two friendly nations. Napoleon didn't declare war on the Ottomans; he just wanted to control Egypt in order to cut off England's trade route to India. England, of course, was his greatest enemy. That was very intelligent, but it didn't work out. You also know that our two nations experienced a period of excellent relations during the reign of Sultan Suleyman the Magnificent. The King of France, François I, and his mother, the Duchess of Dangolen, sent Ambassador Count Jan de Franjipan to request assistance from our Sultan, who obliged unselfishly. Rather than face off against each other because of one emperor, this painting depicts the attitude I much rather hoped would shape today's political relations with yesterday's friendly memories and carry them into the future."

"Mr. Ambassador, are you trying to tell me something, or am I mistaken?"

"No, Excellency, you are not mistaken. I want you to know that I'm very sincere when expressing friendship. Disregard the fact that what I'm about to show you was penned by myself; I was obliged to do this as part of my job. However, because you have shown me such cordiality, I am comfortable discussing a crucial matter with you."

"I'm listening, Mr. Ambassador."

Turning to Zeki, Behic asked for the copy of the previous day's communiqué to Ankara in which Behic suggested retaliation.

"I suppose you're aware of the problems and objections we face regarding the property of our Jewish citizens," Behiç said.

"Yes, and they've told me that you have been rather insistent on the entire issue," replied Laval.

Behiç turned to Zeki and asked him to translate the last paragraph regarding retaliation word for word. As Sedat Zeki spoke, Laval froze, and then he exploded

"We have trade relations going back hundreds of years," he exclaimed.

Behiç nodded his head in agreement "Unfortunately, I know."

"There's also the Ottoman Bank," said Laval.

Again Behiç nodded. "Excellency, we talked about history just now. Well, one of the articles in the Capitulation Treaty, which was signed with France in 1535, regarded the appropriation of very low customs tariffs from French merchants, and another concerned the goods of living or deceased French merchants within Ottoman borders. They were not to be confiscated on behalf of the Sultan, but rather given back to their country, with the Turks on French soil to benefit from the same rights. Another article, which can be put in direct context with our objections here in France, states that the French residing on Ottoman soil could belong to the religion and sect of their choice. In other words, we were not to subject your citizens to any sort of persecution and apply the same treatment and laws to every one of your citizens, not to confiscate your goods, even in cases of deceased merchants, but rather return them to France; and France was going to treat our citizens in the same exact light.

This treaty is the common history of our two countries. My request to you, and I'm being sincere here, is for you to own up to our common history. Both of us know that as a consequence of these agreements, the best interests of France were looked after for hundreds of years, so that today you have important economic benefits in Turkey. We both know that Turkish citizens living here, Jewish or not, possess benefits that are nowhere near the level you have in Turkey. I believe in all sincerity that, as a final resort, retaliation against the French in Turkey should be carried out. As a matter of fact, as the ambassador to France, I wrote Ankara stating that this should be implemented immediately. But in stating my opinions, the voice inside me wants to learn if the President of the Vichy government is willing to remain loyal to that treaty that was amicably signed by our ancestors in the name of good intentions and friendship. Because here within lays the solution to the problem we are facing today. The only thing I want from you is that you own up to your history."

"France is going through some very dark days, Mr. Ambassador, but let me assure you, we haven't forgotten our history and we're not going to forget it, either. I want to express that your personal initiative on behalf of your country's best interests is highly admirable. I don't want any bad blood to exist between the people of two friendly nations. Objections regarding your citizens will be dealt with."

"You are very kind and considerate, thank you very much," said Behiç.

"By the way, when did you send the communiqué you translated for me to Ankara?"

"Yesterday, but don't worry. We're in the midst of a war. Ankara is busy with more pressing matters. It will be some time before we receive a response."

"So, I take it you're also going to notify them of this conversation?"

"I'm going to wait a while and once I obtain some solid results that our problems have been solved, I'll write them, including a couple of actual cases and mentioning the outcome we've reached with you today at the beginning of the memo."

"Fine. Please keep me informed as well, Mr. Ambassador."

Sedat Zeki said that after the French delegation left, he was exuberant and exclaiming "Diplomacy!" Behic said it was not diplomacy but rather, history. He had been studying history and international law for the past week.

"Actually, there were one or two more things I wanted to say, but I couldn't work them in.There was a time when Suleyman the Magnificent saved King François I of France from the German Emperor Charles V, who had razed Europe to the ground, to win the title of Holy Roman Emperor. And another time the Ottoman fleet, under the command of Barbaros, sailed into Marseilles Harbor, captured a few forts from the Spaniards who were the enemies of France, and after spending the winter in Toulon, gave the forts back to the French and returned home. We saved his king, saved his forts and he doesn't even lift a finger for our citizens. Why? Because they're Jewish! You see, in the dictionary the word for that is ingratitude. The Ministry of Foreign Affairs and the Jewish Task Force have been ungrateful since the beginning."

After a moment Zeki asked Behic which Ottoman General that was in the painting.

"You know, I'm not really sure. It was part of the scenario I planned. Thinking it would be necessary to incorporate a visual effect into the history angle, I had Bodo run down to a nearby antique shop and pay a small deposit to borrow the painting. He's going to return it tomorrow!"

It didn't take Ankara four months to respond to the "Let's retaliate" communiqué.

Ankara 10-6-1942
Re: Jewish citizens in France
Ministry of Foreign Affairs   :
U. No. 28420
Ref: 72   Turkish Embassy (Vichy)
Reply to Communiqué No. 597/383/6127, dated 15/5/1942:
Your proposal of retaliation against the French in the event the Vichy Government insists on only allowing observers for our Jewish citizens in France goes against the grain of our general principles regarding the Jewish question. Consequently, we reserve our rights in this matter.

Deputy Vice-Foreign Minister

Since the response was not an out and out no, in diplomatic terms Behic felt it was a successful outcome and informed his ministry as well as giving them the news about President Laval's promise to respect Turkish Jews and their property. As a follow up he sent a memo to the French.

Vichy, 9 July 1942
Re: Our Jewish citizens in France
To the Supreme Ministry of Foreign Affairs

Reply to your decree No. 28420/72 dated 10 June 1942

As a last resort, I discussed the issue of protecting the interests of our Jewish citizens with M. Laval. He stated that he would do his utmost to ensure that Turkish national administrators were appointed to the businesses of Jewish Turks. Moreover, the President of the Vichy Government also confirmed this verbally with M. Rochat and M. Lagarde. Of course, I will submit to you the written reply as soon as it is obtained from the Ministry of Foreign Affairs.

Because the French have been more than a little evasive on this issue up until today, I'm obliged to act more cautiously in order not to accept the situation as completely taken care of without seeing the outcome of the application.

State representatives who haven't accepted any of our preventive measures regarding our Jewish citizens still have not realized their objectives. Additionally, I will inform you of the claims at a later date.

Paris Ambassador
Behiç Erkin

CHOICES TO MAKE

* * *

Behic called a staff meeting to review the situation in which they now found themselves. An enormous map of Europe was spread over his desk.

"The latest news we've been getting is not very pleasant. The Germans have been arresting large numbers of Jews and putting them in camps. The Germans started by destroying the Jewish businesses, but now it looks as if the Germans are intent on going after the Jews themselves. What are they going to do with all these people? It's not even sure where they're sending them. To tell you the truth, I don't have too many clear-cut ideas in my head. You know what we've faced regarding the businesses of our Turkish-Jewish citizens. Imagine what we'll face if we have to sort out thousands of arrests." Pausing to let this sink in a bit he continued.

"I've been studying this map for hours and I've reached some conclusions I want to share with you. Let's first look at Turkey's situation in this war. What's Germany's? What's our situation here? Germany has occupied two-thirds of France, all of Holland, Belgium, Luxemburg, Poland, part of Russia, the Balkans, and Greece. Hitler guaranteed President □nönü that the German army wouldn't come within 85 kilometers of our border. We've no idea how much we can trust him, but the Germans have never sent anyone a written declaration stating that they were attacking. At least, I've never heard of such a thing from the ambassadors whose countries have been occupied. Because the Germans stopped at Turkey's doorstep has made us think we are more valuable to them when compared to everyone else.

Ask yourself this question. Why didn't Hitler march into Turkey? He wasn't afraid of Russia; he didn't fear the 10 or so countries he occupied. So why did he stop when he approached our doorstep and then make a promise not to get any closer? We shouldn't forget that our next-door neighbor Greece surrendered in April last year. In other words, the Germans haven't attacked for almost 18 months. I'm sure they weren't afraid, so why did they stop? I've been contemplating this and have come to the conclusion there were not many reasons.

1- We were Germany's closest ally during World War I. General Enver positioned German officers at the highest levels in our army. Could this be a reason? Perhaps, but it's a weak possibility.

2- Right now Germany has to focus its attention on the lands it occupies making Russia, a large and tough enemy to fight, its most critical front. Turkey has been able to throw out all the armies that ever coveted her territory, a fact that German officers know well since they had commanding positions in our army. The army that picks a fight with us would suffer catastrophic losses. Most likely Hitler doesn't want this.

3- Germany would never want us to join the Allies so, as a political strategy, it would be incorrect to invade us.

4- Turkey accepted Hitler's Non-Aggression Treaty which made the Allied Forces and Hitler has kept his promise for a year and a half. In reality, Hitler made a major commitment with this treaty. Not only does he avoid the risk of dividing his army by attacking us, thus losing strength, he also ruins our relationship with the Allies by having us accept his treaty. Well, this is very intelligent and this is the reason that makes the most sense to me. At least for now!

Remaining neutral is something that President İsmet Inonu has been attempting to do since the beginning which is probably why responses from Ankara to the critical issues we query arrive four months later. The President knows me quite well, and he's probably thinking that I'm doing whatever is necessary.

He knew I didn't appreciate anyone interfering in business and responsibilities I was given. I told Mustafa Kemal that the only way I'd accept the top post at the Railway Administration is if nobody interfered with my work and he accepted that condition. I felt the need to explain this in order for you to understand what I am about to tell you.

Though we're facing fast-breaking developments, I still inform Ankara and request instructions for what needs to be done. As someone who knows Ankara and the workings of the ministry very well, I wire instructions to you and the Consulates without waiting for approval. Usually Ankara doesn't answer, and if they do the message arrives four months after the fact.

Don't ask me what the Turkish Ambassador in Germany is doing or what kind of luck he's having in such proximity to Hitler, but here we are in a constant state of protest against Laval, the number one collaborator of the Germans, and, the Germans themselves!

We walk a fine line by not creating problems for those demanding citizenship yet raising official objections regarding the laws against the Jews. We are in the eye of the storm, penning our signature to communiqués dealing with matters that could inflame the Germans. Our President is pursuing a very intelligent policy. If the tides of war shift within four months, that would give him enough time to refute German claims he sent me such and such orders.

Now that I have made a short story long, let me share with you what we're going to do under these conditions. As long as Turkey doesn't declare war on Germany or vice-versa, Germany will not wish to oppose us here in the embassy, so what we will do is direct our complaints and demands to the German officials. As long as Turkey remains neutral, there is nothing to fear."

While the Turkish diplomats utilized every possible way to successfully resolve the difficulties posed by French and German authorities either amicably or by threatening retaliatory action, hundreds of letters flooded in from Turkish Jews pleading for assistance from the Turkish diplomatic corps.

Le Maison du Bas
Elie Merdjan
2 Rue de la République, Béziers
17 June 1942

Mr. Ambassador of the Turkish Republic, Vichy

Mr. Ambassador,

I the undersigned Merdjan Elie, citizen of the Turkish Republic who entered France on May 16,1931, address myself to Your Excellency, representative of the Turkish Republic, to defend my interests which have been damaged as a result of the laws and measures decreed by the Jewish Task Force. In effect, despite my nationality and my regular contacts with my consulate at Marseilles, an Administrator was assigned to my shop on December 2 ,1941. Since that day I have had no access to my money, my merchandise, and even worse my home where I live with my family. I must draw your attention to the fact that yesterday, Tuesday June 16, 1942, my Administrator verbally warned me that he had received orders to liquidate my business by selling it an auction and that he would come today to evaluate my home, for what purpose I do not know.

Mr. Ambassador, I am the father of a family, born in the heart of Anatolia, in the city of Manisa to a family which has been Turkish for many generations, and where I wish to remain. All my ancestors have always served our country, the last being my father who fought during World War I and I myself participated in the rescue of my country at the time of the Greek invasion despite my youth, in 1921.

Our Republic does not make any difference regarding race or religion, and it is for that reason that I make an urgent appeal to you, Mr. Ambassador, to intervene with authorities concerned with this matter to stop these measures in time. I have never had anyone reproach me in all my 11 years in France. I have carried out my trade with loyalty and honesty and my conduct has been exemplary.

Behiç did intervene by halting the sale of Elie Merdjan's home and business and facilitated the appointment of a Turk to administer Merdjan's business (which meant that he regained control of his own business) and quickly wrote an explanatory letter to Elie Merdjan c/o the Marseilles Consul-General on August 3.

By making it look as though the Germans were responsible for the problems caused to the Jews, the French Government delighted in transferring confiscated Jewish money and assets into their own treasury, while taking an excruciatingly long time to transfer promises they gave the Ambassador on paper.

Finally on July 31, 1942, the French government confirmed that an agreement had been reached regarding non-Jewish Turks as administrators over the businesses, property and goods of Turkish-Jewish citizens, and requested a list of Turkish administrative candidates from the Turkish Embassy to pass on to the Jewish Task Force so they could make the selection.

True, there was some optimism at the Turkish Embassy because businesses were being returned to Turkish control, but information was revealed during these transfers that neither the Consulate-General nor the embassy had known about. Some of the Jewish-owned businesses were being managed by French administrators because their true owners had been sent to Drancy.

Marcel Brunaud, 6, Rue Felix Ziem, Paris XVIII
Ref: Aff Alcabes, No.61.477

To the Attention of the Turkish Consul
170 Boulvard Haussmann, Paris
To the Esteemed Consul-General

I have the honor of informing you that by the decision of the Jewish Task Force, I have been named Provisional Administrator of a bonneterie [department store] belonging to Monsieur Alcabes, 35 Rue St-Sébastien, Paris. Despite the lack of information and the absence of Monsieur Alcabes, who is imprisoned at Drancy, I have just learned that he is of Turkish origin.

Under these conditions, I wish to ask you, if you judge it necessary to name a Provisional Turkish administrator, and I will be happy to get into contact with him to transmit the small amount of documentation that I possess. In awaiting an answer, please accept the expression of my very special sentiments.

The Turkish Consul-General replied in the following:

Paris Turkish Consulate-General
September10, 1942
Mr. Marcel Brunaud, 6 Rue Felix Ziem, Paris 8.

In response to your letter of August 20, 1942 reference Affaire Alcabes No.61477, I wish to inform you that this Consulate-General will immediately undertake the necessary efforts to nominate a Turkish administrator for the firm of Monsieur Alcabes, a Turkish citizen who is regularly registered at this Consulate-General.

Please accept my special greetings,

The Consul-General (signed)

P.S. Monsieur Alcabes is no longer imprisoned at Drancy, but is now at his home.

FRANCE UNDER OCCUPATION

* * *

The Nazis continued to finalize their plans of transferring Jews from France to concentration camps in the east which was not an easy task. Dispatching the Jewish-filled trains from France to Poland meant they would have to travel through much of Europe, calling for a very complicated and difficult organization. Timing and coordination had to be perfect or else the wagons would be carrying dead Jews instead of live Jews and although the final solution was to exterminate all Jews, the Germans did need live ones for slave labor in their war industries.

When a train was off schedule on July 15, 1942, Eichmann became furious. He telephoned the *Judenreferat* in Paris to deliver a protest that must have greatly upset Heinz Röthke, the new man in charge.

The SS Obersturmführer (Eichmann) pointed out that it was a matter of prestige; difficult negotiations had been successfully conducted with the Reich Transport Ministry for these convoys, and now Paris was canceling a train! Such a thing had never happened to him before. The whole affair was disgraceful.

Toforce the issue Eichmann made his ultimate threat to Röthke: perhaps Hitler should drop France entirely as a country to be evacuated, thus denying France the privilege of being Jew-free. Thrown on the defensive, Röthke begged Eichmann not to do so, and promised all future deportations would leave on time.

Beginning on August 24, 1942, the German occupation forces began putting all Jews over the age of 18 who had immigrated to France during the previous 20 years into French concentration camps like Drancy or to those at Compiegne and Vernet. Having taken census, they already had all the facts about the French Jews and could find them easily. Later, generally within a month, the Jews would be shipped east where most would be quickly exterminated.

Despite the fact that the Jewish Turks insisted they were Turkish citizens, they, too, were generally rounded up and some were dispatched with the others. As soon as a relative contacted the Turkish Embassy or one of the Consulates, an all-out effort was made by the Turkish authorities to free those who had been whisked off in this fashion. However, if no one reported them missing, as was the case with more than 1,600 Turkish Jews, the diplomats could not save them.

During the first two years of occupation, the French and German authorities accepted the Certificates of Citizenship prepared by the Turkish Embassy and Consulates. During those two years, the Germans also noticed the steadily growing numbers of Jews in front of the Turkey's Embassy and Consulates.

In November of 1942, the Germans began scrutinizing the Turkish Certificates of Citizenship more carefully. When the Vichy government began collaborating more earnestly, Vallat (head of the Jewish Task Force) noticed there were some Jews who had failed to maintain their Turkish citizenship. Recognizing there was no dual citizenship legislation possible, he had a list prepared of all Jews who were French citizens in 1940 but declared themselves Turkish citizens in the census count conducted in the Unoccupied Zone in 1941.

By comparing the names registered in the census records with those from the Jewish census count, Vallat noticed that there were around 10,000 Jews living in the Unoccupied Zone who registered themselves as Turkish citizens in 1941 but were French citizens in 1940. This explained why there were so many Jews in front of the Turkish Embassy and Consulates. Immediately, Vallat told the Germans what he had learned and the pressure on the Turkish legation to save Turk'sh Jews increased.

THE BIG PLANS

* * *

Because my grandfather remembered the Turkish commanders who in recent wars ordered their own men to to fight to death thereby freeing their land from the grip of the enemy, he was unable to comprehend how the French could surrender their country without fighting to the last drop of blood. Behic took great pride in a history that conveyed the true meaning of the word "homeland;" a land that people were willing to defend to death.

In this context, he was absolutely determined to protect everyone with an identification card bearing the crescent moon and star, who considered Turkey to be their motherland, irrespective of their religion, race, or language. Although he dispensed instructions expediently, the incidents of detention became his most significant concern and caused the lives of his Turkish diplomats to be stressed and more problematic by the day.

But Behiç had a plan. It was a plan fraught with danger; a plan that could cost the lives of all those involved. For this reason, he studied it methodically, not rushing into anything. He had to be careful and patient because there was too much at stake. In April of 1942 in Communiqué No. 270/6127 addressed to Marseilles Consul-General Bedi'i Arbel, Behiç asked a few questions that had been on his mind.

What routes could be used for sending Jews to Turkey? What sort of difficulties would "irregular Turkish citizens" face regarding military service in Turkey?

Bedi'i Arbel responded that the best way was by rail just as they had previously sent students in 1940/1941.

The Nazis began sending Jews who had immigrated to France from Poland, Czechoslovakia, Germany, Austria, and Russia to Auschwitz. The French took all children under 18 from their parents and sent the children to welfare homes. All those Jews over the age of 18 were loaded onto the trains and sent east. They shut people into cattle cars with no food, only a bucket of water, and a barrel in which they were to empty their urine and feces,sending them on like freight.

The trains were often en route for 20 days, going from Unoccupied France through Germany, and then over to Auschwitz in Poland. Those who were still alive after such a journey were either selected for slave labor or exterminated.

On 1 September 1942 French general Mougin, France's representative to Ankara during the War of Liberation, paid Behiç a visit. During the meeting he related a recent incident that involved some Jews at a French train station, There was a mother with her infant waiting at the station to be loaded onto a railcar and deported to Poland. As the authorities were trying to extricate her baby from her arms, she pleaded with a French police officer to let her nurse her baby one last time. Then she pressed her baby against her breast, suffocating it by sheer force. Visibly shaken the French police officer quickly retreated from the scene.

Communiqué No. 1197/770 to Ankara described the inhumane circumstances the Jews were now facing and included General Mougin's recollection of the horrible scene he witnessed at the train station. This communiqué underscored the heart wrenching eternal separation of a mother and her baby and went beyond Behiç's official capacity as ambassador.

In his memoirs, Behiç explained that he came up with an idea that could save the Turkish Jews and touched upon the matter during his weekly meeting with the Foreign Affairs Undersecretary Rochat. He told Rochat that he wanted to send those Turkish citizens who so desired back to Turkey and furthermore he wanted Rochat's help putting the plan together. It took a few moments before the shock of the request wore off but Rochat doubted the feasibility of the plan especially since most of the people were Jewish. Besides, even if the French gave their permission, the Germans probably would not.

"If I get immediate permission from the Germans, would you give us the needed approval?"

"The Germans wouldn't grant permission, you'd be wasting your time. However, if they did, then I cannot say that we wouldn't grant permission."

"Fine." And Behic headed back to his embassy.

Immediately he requested an appointment with Krug von Nidda who said that the matter exceeded his authority but he would discuss the situation with the necessary offices and get back to him. A few days later, von Nidda informed Behiç that an appointment was arranged for the following morning with his uperiors but he would only learn of the place at the last minute. As soon as von Nidda learned where the meeting was to take place, he would pick up Behiç at the Turkish Embassy and take him to that address.

Early the next morning, von Nidda picked up Behiç and Sedat Zeki and they headed off in the direction of Paris. After about 200 kilometers, they were met by a German military vehicle and the three men changed vehicles. After riding for about 20 minutes, they stopped in front of an old French chateau. While the von Nidda went to talk to the guard on duty, Sedat Zeki, who was obviously very nervous asked Behic how he always managed to maintain his composure.

"Are you serious? I'm half expecting these Germans will kill us after I present them with my request. Does that help your nerves?"

A Nazi soldier led the three men to a room upstairs. The curtains in this high-ceiling room were closed making it dark and difficult to see the faces of the German officers waiting for them. One was seated at a table; the other two were standing on either side of the table which was covered with a large map. Von Nidda made the introductions and then it was my grandfather's turn.

"I'm here in the capacity of the ambassador of the Republic of Turkey. Since it is obvious that this war is going to continue longer than first expected, I am planning to send my citizens who want to return, back to Turkey. However..."

"Perhaps you're talking about your Jews, Mr. Ambassador?" interrupted the officer who was seated.

"You're planning to send Jews?" another one asked incredulously.

One thing I can say from my own experiences, Grandpa Behic did not like being interrupted.

"Since I know *exactly* what I am talking about, perhaps *you* didn't quite understand, so allow me to explain. I'm going to give Turkish citizens presently living in France the opportunity to return to Turkey. However, since every country they must pass through is under German occupation, I would appreciate it if you would approve this matter and provide free passage."

"Why would we want to approve of such a situation, Mr. Ambassador?"

"There are two reasons. First, there is the historical relationship between our countries when Turkey was the German Empire's most important ally during World War I. If you can recall those days, two of your warships took shelter in our straits and while we came to your rescue, they had the audacity to bomb some Russian harbors, thus dragging us into the war. Though Germany lost the war on her own territory, we won the war on our land. But because we were your ally, we had no choice but to sit at the table with all the defeated parties. As a result of our alliance with you, we lost a lot of territory even though we won *our* war. If you admit to the historical reality, you have an obligation to pay to an old friend and ally and it is time to settle up. That's the first reason. Now for as the second reason..."

Behiç paused, removed something from the left pocket of his jacket, went over to the table and placed it in front of the German officer sitting there.

"While I'm submitting my request to you as the ambassador of a friendly nation, the person standing in front of you is one who was found deserving enough by your German Emperor to be awarded the country's highest honor, the Iron Cross, 1st Degree . So, it is on the merit of these two very compelling reasons that you must give me permission!"

When Sedat Zeki told this story years later, he said you could hear a pin drop in the room. "Alright, we'll let you do this, provided it is completed by the end of this year," said the seated officer.

"No, that's impossible. It's going to take a lot longer to complete all this business."

"Okay, we'll let you know about the deadline later."

"I was certain you weren't going to ignore the historical friendship of our two countries. I congratulate you and thank you."

As they got into the car, Zeki whispered to Behic that he had been praying silently throughout the entire meeting and Behic whispered back that so had he!

"Now I understand why you didn't tell me what you were going to talk about!"

"If I had told you, I would have had to come here on my own."

"Why is that?"

"You would have been too afraid to come along or you would have found an excuse."

"When duty calls, sir, it is unavoidable."

"I still don't think you would have come along."

"Truthfully, I would have because I wanted to see what kind of diplomatic tactics you were going to use on these Germans!"

"That wasn't diplomacy, Sedat Zeki. I was working out this plan in my head for the past two months. Since my job in both the Battle for Gallipoli during War World I and the War of Liberation was to ensure the consignments of soldiers and supplies to the front by using only the railroads, for the past two months I was wracking my brain about how to make a proposal using what I know best."

"You planned it out perfectly."

"I didn't plan it."

"But you just said, you had been contemplating it for the past two months."

"I was thinking about it, but I didn't say that I created a plan."

"Fine, but what was all that you said to the Germans?"

"I just thought it all up in the room."

"But what about the medal?"

"I thought that up in the room, too."

"But if you didn't plan that, what was the medal doing in your pocket?"

"I brought it along thinking it might save me in case I was thrown into one of their camps after making my demands."

"Then what was going to become of me, Mr. Ambassador?"

"Didn't you tell me you were reciting the *Kelime-i* şahadet to God? So what could you possibly hope for from me when you've got Him?"

"Who were those Germans we talked with?"

"I don't know."

"You didn't recognize any of them?"

"No."

"Weren't they introduced to us?"

"I was too nervous. I didn't pay attention to their names. I was still thinking about what to say!"

Later von Nidda told them they had met with Otto Abetz, Rudolf Schleier and Heinz Röthke.

Actually, the Germans may have accepted my grandfather's request because it suited their own interests. More than 150,000 Jews who registered during Xavier Vallat's census had fled to the Unoccupied Zone. This exodus of Jews continued despite all the measures implemented by the Germans to stop them. The Germans were now faced with an immense problem of trying to find all these Jews who had left. Rounding up even half of the 330,000 Jews living all over France, placing them in concentration camps, then deporting them by rail across France to Poland would take not only great logistics but more manpower than Vichy France possessed at the time. In non-compliance with the law, the Turkish Embassy would not allow its Jewish citizens to be moved into walled ghettoes in both the Occupied Zone as well as the Unoccupied Zone. What frustrated the Germans the most was the persistence and ability of the Turkish Consulate-General staff in Paris to track down Jewish Turks who had been detained in the French concentration camps.

The round-up of Jews continued even though the Germans had accepted Behiç's demands. On September 7, Otto Abetz asked Berlin if he could send 3,046 Jewish Turks that had remained in the Paris area to the camps. On September 19, a message addressed to the Turkish Government arrived from Martin Luther an official at the anti-Semitic Foreigners' Bureau in Berlin.

Due to military reasons, all Jews in the west shall comply with all the measures to be implemented against the other Jews. For this reason, the Turkish Government has until January 31 ,1943, to evacuate its Jewish citizens from occupied territory, whereupon no such privileges will be afforded after that date.

Signed,
LUTHER

It is fair to assume that it was due to the persistenceof the Turkish ambassador who was adamant about protecting the rights of his Jewish citizens, on September12, 1942 the German government, authorized the Vichy government and French officials to let the countries of Holland, Belgium, Italy, Turkey, Switzerland, Spain, Portugal, Denmark, Sweden, Finland, Hungary and Romania evacuate their Jewish citizens from Occupied and Unoccupied France, with a deadline set for 31 January 1943, after which all Jews remaining would be subject to the same anti-Jewish regulations regardless of nationality.

The Ambassador's continuous efforts to protect his Jewish citizens through official communiqués with the French Ministry of Foreign Affairs, the Germans, and even with Vichy President Laval became known throughout the Turkish-Jewish community in France. Behiç responded to every letter addressed to him, assisted everyone who knocked on his door. But one of the most critical issues was that he supported the irregular Turks, those who emigrated to France decades earlier and had even forgotten how to speak Turkish.

On October 30,1942, Behiç received a letter from Mr. Yakar, the head of the Turkish-Jewish community in France:

For your eyes only   10.30.1942

To His Excellency Behiç Erkin, Our Vichy Ambassador;

We are grateful to you for allowing us to send the petition we wrote to President İsmet İnönü in order to explain the matter regarding the Turkish-Jewish population who are of Turkish descent but who have not maintained their registration on a regular basis in compliance with the deportation law which is enforced in France. We learned with great satisfaction of the role undertaken by your Embassy and the great efforts exerted regarding the assistance afforded to the Jews.

All the senior citizens, women, children, the disabled, and poor citizens in our patronage offer you a prayer of good fortune on behalf of all our fellow non-registered Jews with all our hearts.

The exalted heart and soul of Behiç, who has lessened the burden of households, who has lessened the pain of the miserable and wretched survivors like us and who has acknowledged our appeal for assistance during this unmitigated disaster which we find ourselves in today, one that is rarely found in the pages of history. He who conducts beneficent work, of course, garners accolades and deserves such accolades.

May God Bless Our Ambassador along with all the members of his family and keep them in good health and spirits, Amen.

Our Exalted Ambassador, please accept our highest respects.

On behalf of the thousands of poor, irregular Jewish Turks living in France.

B2142
Yakar[6]

---

6   The original copy of this letter is preserved in the İnkilap Tarih Müzesi (Revolution History Museum), on the premises of the Turkish Revolution Institution at Ankara University. It is registered in Catalogue Tite-A6, Row No.113, Box No.190 with the entry, "Letter written on behalf of our Jewish citizens in France."

When President İnönü showed the letter which arrived from the Chairman of the Jewish community in France to the Minister of Foreign Affairs, Numan Menemencioğlu, who had questioned the President's choice for ambassador, he asked two questions.

"Do you know why Atatürk, Behiç's close friend, presented him with the surname of 'Erkin' in his own handwriting?"

"No I don't," said Minister Numan.

"Because Erkin means 'independent;' it means 'one who has the courage to take the initiative, regardless of the prevailing conditions.' That is what independence is all about. Now do you understand why I thought Behiç was the right person for that job in France?"

The first train filled with Turkish Jews and draped with the Turkish flag left the station from Paris on November, 1942. Among those on board was Lazare Rousso The trip to Turkey took eleven days and a Consulate-General official accompanied the passengers during the entire trip. Some of the passengers had nicknamed the trains "The Ambassador's Trains," but the Turkish Embassy staff called them "Behiç's Trains."

During his journey to Turkey, Lazare Rousso couldn't stop thinking about the trains of cattle cars rushing past them. He knew that they were filled with Jews headed towards the concentration camps while his train, full of Jews, was headed towards freedom. When the train reached Edirne, a Turkish town near the Bulgarian border, a Turkish soldier boarded the train and suddenly a lady started screaming at the top of her lungs, "We're in Turkey, we've been saved!"

Back in France, my grandfather was surprised to learn that the Vichy government objected to the short deadline the Germans had set to evacuate the Jews. Then he found out that Pierre Laval had lodged a personal objection because he felt the Jewish deportation would adversely affect French businesses which utilized Jewish laborers.

On the morning of November 11, Behiç was headed to a meeting at the Park Hotel with Undersecretary Rochat when, as he approached the hotel, he saw German soldiers and officers waiting in several cars and trucks directly in front of the hotel. Entering Rochat's office, Behic learned he would be meeting with Rochat's assistant, Lagarde. Lagarde told Behiç that the Germans crossed the line that was agreed upon in the armistice with the intentions of occupying all of France. On November 16, Fikret Şefik Özdoganci, Cevdet Dülger's replacement as Consul-General in Paris, sent a communiqué to Behic containing a frank assessment of the "irregular" Turkish Jews and their situation in the Paris area where most lived.

THE TURKISH CONSULATE GENERAL
PARIS   Paris, 11.16.1942

Your Excellency Behiç Erkin
Our Esteemed Ambassador and Chief
Vichy

Since my arrival in Paris, I have desired to personally present my respects to your exalted offices. Actually, as soon as I handled some Consulate-related affairs in Paris as well as some matters concerning Mr. Numan Menemencioğlu in Ankara, I received permission to come to Vichy. However, I encountered a lot of work that has piled up here. In particular, matters surrounding the irregular Jews constitute the greater part of the workload at the Consulate-General.

In light of the current extraordinary situation, I find it necessary to get involved in their matters and if the opportunity presents itself, to settle them as soon as possible.

However, despite the fact we work day and night on these matters, the end is nowhere in sight.

The purpose of submitting these matters is that I wish to be pardoned by you for any mistakes I have possibly made.

Signed,
Fikret Şefik Özdoganci

The problems in Vichy were ceaseless. Even though the Germans gave the Vichy Government permission to quickly evacuate the Jews, the Vichy Government decided to reverse that decision by stopping the French Interior Ministry from issuing exit visas although they never canceled the original resolution. Thus the evacuation came to a grinding halt.

My grandfather went into action again on November 24 with Communiqué No.1532-6127 to the French Ministry of Foreign Affairs:

The Embassy of Turkey presents its compliments to the Ministry of Foreign Affairs and has the honor of informing it that, according to information sent by the Turkish Consulate-General in Marseilles, the competent French authorities have been refusing exit visas to Turkish citizens desiring to return to Turkey, on the basis of an order given them by the Ministry of the Interior. Such a measure can have grave consequences for those involved, and greatly complicates the task of that Consulate. The Embassy cannot conceive of the legality of such a measure and believes that an error of interpretation has occurred. It asks the Ministry of Foreign Affairs therefore to study this problem as a matter of urgency.

Meanwhile, Bedi'i Arbel, Marseilles Consul, brought another problem to the attention of the Turkish ambassador. The level of cruelty against the Jews had reached new heights increasing the number of applicants from Turkish Jews wishing to return to Turkey. Not only were the exit visas from the French Interior Ministry a problem, but obtaining visas from countries they would have to travel through was creating another difficult situation. They would be able to work with those countries that had maintained contact with the Consulate but what were they supposed to do regarding those countries with whom no diplomatic relations existed? Turkish Jews returning to Turkey could face real danger.

Bedi'i Arbel, wanted instructions from Behiç Erkin regarding all the visa forms and suggested that advertisements could be placed in the Marseilles, Nice and Lyon newspapers to let "Turks" know it was now possible to return home. Behiç approved of the idea and applications greatly increased as a result.

THE SLAUGHTERHOUSE

* * *

Upset by the German advancement into the Unoccupied Zone, Behic went to discuss the situation with von Nidda, Behiç was given some bac news. When Berlin was informed of the meeting in the countryside between Behic and von Nidda's superiors, Adolf Eichmann had a fit in Berlin. He felt that Behic was protecting Jews and although the trains were allowed to depart for Turkey, instructions arrived about Behic, personally.

"Since our old ally, Turkey, is maintaining its neutral stance in this war, it is not deemed necessary to take measures related to the Turkish Ambassador at this time, but his embassy activities must be closely monitored."

Behiç's trademark smile crossed his face as he thanked von Nidda for sharing that bit of information. There was one more bit of information for the Ambassador. The Germans planned to set up surveillance operations in the building adjacent to the embassy.

Returning to the embassy Behic informed a bewildered Sedat Zeki that they were going to visit the local slaughterhouse the next day but he never explained why. When they arrived at the slaughterhouse, Behiç asked to speak with the manager. Introducing himself, Behic spoke with the manager for a while and made a specific request.

"Do you have anyone here that fits the description?"

"Yes, sir…André… André Picard. I'll have him come in here so you can see for yourself."

A giant of a man wearing a blood stained leather apron and blood spotted knee-high leather boots appeared in the doorway. In his hand he held a super-sized meat cleaver covered in fresh blood.

Andre looked puzzled. He had no idea why the two men in suits were in his boss's office and why he had been called in. When Andre spoke, his voice was as imposing as his appearance.

"He's just what we're looking for. I'm the Turkish ambassador, and I want to make you a job offer. I'll pay you three times what you earn here if you'll accept employment as the embassy's doorman."

"Three times my salary?"

"Yes. But you'll have two important responsibilities. Hundreds of our Turkish citizens, mainly Jewish, visit our embassy every day to get documents. We are glad to see them and want to help them, but there are so many that there is often an overflow at the gate and inside on the stairs. One of your jobs will be to maintain order. Your second duty is one of humanity and conscience. Sooner or later, the Germans, who are setting up a surveillance post in the building next door, will conduct a raid on the embassy because of our activities with our Jewish citizens. When that day comes, you must lean your massive body against the gate to give us time to do what we have to do in the boiler room."

André Picard didn't quite comprehend what this bald-headed old man, leaning on a cane, wanted of him. But there was one thing Andre did understand and he wanted to make sure about it.

"You just said three times the salary I earn here, didn't you, Monsieur?"

"Yes, exactly three times."

"Alright, you've got yourself a deal."

Behiç on duty...

A few days later, Emine, an embassy clerk's wife, was startled by a loud commotion coming from the ground floor of the Vichy hotel where she and her husband had a room. The shouting and screaming in German was coming up the stairwell. Just then, somebody pounded on Emine's door and peering through the peephole, she saw the Mexican ambassador's son who looked absolutely terrified. Since she and her husband were friendly with the boy's father, Emine opened the door.

The young man had a rifle in his hands and with the shouting and screaming getting closer, he begged Emine to hide it for him because he knew the Germans would never bother the Turkish embassy staff. Quickly, Emine grabbed the rifle from the boy and hid it under her bed. Then she grabbed all her I.D. documents and headed for the door. After locking her door, she turned to find a German soldier watching her.

The soldier shouted at her in German so she immediately showed him her papers while repeating that she was Turkish. As the soldier looked through her papers he kept speaking to her in German while other soldiers ran past them through the corridor then up the stairs to the next floor. Emine was having a difficult time communicating until a French-speaking German officer appeared and told her he wanted to take a look in her room from the doorway, without entering. Emine feared the officer could hear her heart pounding and see her legs shaking but she really had no choice so she opened her door. The German poked his head in to get a quick look around, thanked her, and then went upstairs to join the other soldiers.

Emine locked her door and hurried down the stairs. There were German soldiers everywhere as she left the hotel and headed for the Turkish embassy which, thankfully, was close by. Approaching the embassy, Emine noticed that apart from the throng of Jews at the gate, there was a new addition...an enormous doorman. Emine introduced herself as embassy clerk Melih's wife and asked if he would bring him to the gate. When Melih arrived, he took one look at his wife and became concerned because she was still shaking and looked as though she had seen a ghost. Trying to catch her breath, Emine explained that the Germans were conducting a raid at the hotel, checking all the rooms. Then she told him about the rifle.

Melih told his wife to wait there while he went to talk to the Ambassador. A few minutes later he returned and took his wife down the basement stairs to the boiler room where Behic was sitting by himself with a blanket over his knees. He started telling her about an experience he had with Atatürk hoping that would calm her down a bit. He chatted on sharing an amusing memory and it did relax Emine until he finished the story and she realized that she was sitting in the embassy boiler room with the ambassador and the furnace doors were open. Hanging from hooks all over the walls were string bags, the kind used in Europe for grocery shopping, overflowing with papers, documents!

"Mr. Ambassador is it so cold in your office that you have to sit down here?"

"No, young lady. It's my turn to stand watch, that's why I'm here. I've got one more hour to go."

Emine looked confused so he explained that the bags contained documents concerning Jewish Turkish citizens, some of whom don't even speak Turkish. These documents would be very valuable to the Germans. They will probably raid the embassy one day since they have set up surveillance next door. Should that happen, the new doorman will lean against the door to give the staff enough time to incinerate all the bags. Hopefully that will save many people from a certain horrible fate.

The ambassador readjusted the blanket over his knees.

"Everyone on my staff must stand equal watch and when I wrote my own name down for the first watch everyone looked at this dreadfully boring task a little differently. I had just one condition; that I stand watch during the day and because of my age, rather than the standard four-hour stint, I would be down here for two hours.

Nobody objected. That's what I meant by, 'one hour to go on my watch.'"

On December 1, German soldiers and police occupied part of the *Ottoman Bankası* building in Paris, detaining the bank manager. Immediately, my grandfather went over to the adjacent Nazi headquarters to have a word with von Nidda about it and a few days later the Germans left the bank. Behic noted in his memoirs that this was probably meant to annoy and harass since nothing else was done in the building.

The number of rescue operations that began with Lazare Rousso increased dramatically over the ensuing months and years. There was one incident in which the call for help came in the form of a letter. Written by a detainee at Drancy, it was smuggled out of the camp and miraculously reached the Consulate.

Albert Gattegno, explained he was at Drancy, Registry # 15243, Block # 5, Stairs # 22 and Room # 19. In his letter he wrote that two French policemen had come to his home on Tuesday, August 4, at 8:00 a.m. took him to Drancy and his wife Lily to Tourelles without giving any explanation for their arrest, separating them from their two small children. After reading the letter, the Consul-General wrote to Otto Abetz, and the Tourelles Camp Superintendent requesting them to release this husband and wife. Although Lily and Alberto Gattegnos were released the same month, three months later they were rearrested and this time both were sent to Drancy. Again the lengthy process of writing communiqués began. This time it took six weeks to have them released and the Turkish Consulate-General took the extra step of making sure that the French police removed the seals from their home.

THE CODE OF REVENGE

* * *

As 1942 came to a close, the French government began to round up unemployed foreign Jews and transport them to French concentration camps, now euphemistically called Foreign Labor Force Battalions. Newspapers and street posters announced that all unemployed foreign Jews were to immediately register at their local police station. My grandfather noted that this was the revenge the Germans were waiting for; something that could be used against the foreign embassies and especially the Turkish Embassy. Under the guise 'They're already unemployed, let's put them to work' the French and Germans could use the opportunity to add the foreign Jews to the French and German Jews already in the camps. Unfortunately, most neutral countries such as Spain and Switzerland did not object even if they did see through the ruse but Behic was able to crack this code of deception almost immediately.

By now, Otto Abetz had fallen out of favor in Berlin for consistently defending French Admiral Darlan High Commissioner of North Africa as a "friend of the Germans." It didn't help when Darlan surrendered to the Allies in November of 1942 and then agreed to help the Americans. Behiç wondered if another reason for Abetz's downfall was his acceptance of the Turkish Ambassador's evacuation proposal. Right after Abetz agreed to Behic's railroad evacuation plan, the Turkish Embassy received word from President İnönü that the Germans and French had demanded Ambassador Behiç Erkin's recall.

President Inonu rejected this demand but both he and Behiç knew the Ambassador's future in France was under a dark cloud. It was then that my grandfather understood the heavy toll some Germans paid for allowing Turkish Jews to return to Turkey. The Turkish Embassy was always the first embassy to lodge objections and the most persistent protester. The political chess game being played had the Germans on one side and the Turkish Embassy on the other. The Nazis had officially declared that Turkish Jews could return to Istanbul but they created a bureaucratic obstacle by allowing the French to round up foreign Jews for "work camps."

Behic believed this law was devised to retaliate against him, personally. As it was, according to the official registry of the French Government Ministry of Foreign Affairs, every day there were fewer countries with diplomatic missions in France. Countries such as Brazil, Finland, the Dominican Republic, Portugal, Argentina, Bulgaria, Ecuador, Mexico, Colombia, Nicaragua, Cuba, and Chile were not involved with this matter of the Jews. Even if one added up the total number of Jews from all these countries who resided in France, they wouldn't amount to one-twentieth of the approximately 20,000 Turkish Jews. Although the Brazilian Ambassador consulted with Behiç on a regular basis about what the Turkish Embassy was doing concerning their Jewish citizens, Brazil had practically no Jews in France.

Convinced that the compulsory work battalions for the unemployed was the German's idea, Behic went to see Undersecretary Rochat.

"It's been over a year since you fired Jews from all civil service jobs. You've confiscated the few Jewish owned businesses, made all of them officially unemployed by appointing temporary administrators, and liquidated their property by auctioning it off. To date, only 21 foreign countries remain diplomatically accredited in France. Among these, we're the one that lodges the most objections because Turkey's is the only neutral country with a large number of Jewish citizens! Do me a favor; line up all these realities and you'll see that with this law, you are really targeting only Turkey. Why are you doing this despite our good relations? I don't think you want to deliberately derail our bilateral relations, do you?"

Nodding at every point made, Rochat blurted out that the Germans made them do it putting the squeeze on the French. Rochat knew it was aimed at the Turkish Jews.

"Their goal is to get you to round up all the Jews for them, the Germans. They let you take a few to toil on your road projects, but they will take most of them, saying, 'We need workers more than you do,' and then transport them to their own concentration camps. Don't fall for it. It's nothing but a decoy!

These Germans want to take their revenge on me. However, it has to be through official channels so as not to ruin their relationship with Turkey. So they are using you as the intermediary and although they officially approved, in reality they did not ! Although there have been a few train loads of Jews to Turkey, my embassy and consulates have had to put all of their normal business aside to deal with these bureaucratic difficulties. In fact, once I was even forced to say 'Let the citizens take the matter as far as they can, then we can take over from there.'

It's getting to the point where we're starting to resemble a bunch of chickens running around with their heads cut off, dealing with the problems concerning my citizens: saving their businesses; getting their homes unsealed; freeing them from the camps by writing communiqués and personally dealing with camp officials; organizing train trips to Turkey after dealing with bureaucratic problems regarding exit visas as well as the transit visas of other countries.

I'm going to lodge a serious protest against this law because it is such a blatant trap. I'll be providing my Consulates clear and definite instructions regarding this matter as soon as I return to the embassy. I've managed to make it this far and I have no intention of handing over even one person to the Germans or the French while they insist on pushing their compulsory labor battalion nonsense."

There was nothing Rochat could do and they both knew it. Immediately Behic telephoned the Paris and Marseilles Consulates explaining everything. The "foreign Jews" meant not only the 3,046 Turkish Jews living in and around Paris, but also approximately 13,000 Turkish Jews living in the Unoccupied Zone. Then there were the "regular Jews" who never relinquished their Turkish citizenship. By including all those numbers there were at least 20,000 regular and irregular Turkish Jews throughout France.

In a protest note lodged with the French Ministry of Foreign Affairs on December 15, 1942, Behiç accused the French Government of carrying out discriminatory actions.

The Jewish Turks are under the organized protection of the Consulate-General and it is for this reason they must be kept exempt from the unemployed foreign Jewish work groups in France. The Turkish Ambassador considers this practice a grave attack on the rights and most important best interests of Turkish citizens living in France. Due to the urgency of this matter, our Embassy demands the intervention of the French Ministry of Foreign Affairs' authorities at the highest level to ensure that the our Turkish citizens be rendered exempt from this arbitrary action they feel threatened by at this time.

Behiç also informed Ankara of the situation on the same day via Communiqué No. 1667-1054-6127.

I sent the French Ministry of Foreign Affairs a telegram demanding that our Turkish-Jewish citizens not be included in the decision to organize groups of workers comprised of all the unemployed foreign Jews. There is a strong possibility that the French will not extend any immunity. It is for this reason that it is possible we will receive a negative response to our request.

Behiç Erkin

INSTRUCTIONS TO HIS CONSULATES

* * *

When Behiç telephoned the Marseilles and Paris Consulates explaining the true reason behind the law, he told them verbally as well as in subsequent written memos what had to be done.

Marseilles Consul-General Bedi'i Arbel implemented the instructions immediately placing young Vice-Consul Necdet Kent in charge. Necdet Kent met with the Governor of Alpes-Maritimes explaining their stance on exempting Turkish Jews from these practices and why the situation was so sensitive.

The Marseilles Consul sent the Governor of Alpes-Maritimes in Nice Communiqué No. 649/80 on December 17, 1942.

Turkish Consul-General, Marseilles
17 December 1942, No.649/80

To the Esteemed Governor,

I am presenting you with a copy of the letter I sent to the Governor of the Bouches-du-Rhone Region concerning the written decree published in the newspapers pertaining to the compulsory employment of all Jews regardless of nationality. By trusting in your everyday common sense, I am requesting you to apply exemption status for the Jews who are Turkish citizens until a compromise has been reached between the two countries. I've assigned Vice-Consul Necdet Kent to establish direct contact with you to discuss the matter. I trust that you'll provide him with a positive answer. Due to the serious nature of this matter, I hope he will obtain a satisfying outcome from the consultation with you.

Bedi'i Arbel

The Governor sent Bedi'i Arbel a reply on December 19.

To the Esteemed Consul-General,

In reply to your letter dated December17,and subsequent to the discussions I had with Vice-Consul Kent, I wish to inform you that I contacted government officials regarding Turkish-Jewish citizens in the disposition of the matter concerning appropriation and utilization of all Jews to cover the foreign labor deficit of firms. I am awaiting instructions from my government and have since halted these practices against your citizens on a temporary basis.

Signed: The Governor

This was an admission proving that the Turkish Ambassador had been right.

On January 13, 1943, the French Ministry of Foreign Affairs sent Communiqué No. 101 to the Turkish Embassy regarding these problems. The last paragraph read:

To avoid the application of these measures to Turkish citizens, the Ministry of Foreign Affairs would be disposed to look favorably on the return of the interested parties to their countries of origin. In general, the Ministry of Foreign Affairs would be happy to examine with the Embassy of Turkey the conditions necessary to secure repatriation of Jewish Turks desiring to avoid the measures being imposed against foreign Jews.

Nevertheless, when Behic read this in the report sent by the Marseilles Consul-General, he became angry.

"The French are driving us crazy with the things they are doing. We just want to send our citizens home and save them from this uncertain environment. The French government says, 'Get permission from the Germans and we'll let you go.' But look what the Marseilles Consul just sent us! Nine of our Turkish citizens living in the Old Harbor district were taken from their homes and sent to a concentration camp. If the Vichy Government was working properly, we wouldn't have to deal with these incidents of people thrown into concentration camp almost daily I think *our friends* are pleased the Germans keep them propped up in their seats; they don't have a care in the world because they're not Jewish. I wonder if they know the final destination of those taken from the concentration camps by train."

Behiç sent the French Ministry of Foreign Affairs Communiqué No. 175-6127, dated January 3,1943:

To the Ministry of Foreign Affairs

We present the Ministry of Foreign Affairs with information from a report prepared by our Marseilles Consul General and sent to the Turkish Embassy. The report indicates that a number of our Turkish citizens were taken from their homes and sent to concentration camps during an operation conducted in the Old Harbor district.

The names and addresses of these people have been presented in the following list.

Our Embassy will be grateful if your Ministry intervenes and ensures the release of these citizens as well as other Turkish citizens in this situation.

Turkish Ambassador Behiç Erkin

List of those arrested in the Old Harbor District
Name and Surname/Birthplace / Year of Birth/ Address
Ester Kamhi / Istanbul, 1921 / 3 Rue Nationale, Marseilles
Sol Kamhi / Istanbul, 1922 / 3 Rue Nationale, Marseilles
Mathilda Benadava / İzmir, 1909 / Hotel Atlantic, Marseilles
İsak Avimelah / Istanbul, 1885 / 44 Rue Thubaneau, Marseilles
Yeshua Avimelah / Istanbul, 1919 / 44 Rue Thubaneau, Marseilles
Rachel Hasit / Istanbul, 1922 / 4 Rue Mazagaran, Marseilles
Lazar Hasit / Istanbul, 1880 / 4 Rue Mazagaran, Marseilles
Kadın Avimelah / Istanbul, 1920 / 44 Rue Thubaneau , Marseilles
İlya Arditti / Istanbul, 1920 / 13 Rue d'Aubagne, Marseilles

Shortly after the Ambassador wrote to the Ministry to intervene, one of the many reports arrived.

Several Jews, including Turkish-Jewish citizens, were arrested in Marseilles on the nights of January 22 and 23. At first, they were placed in the Beaumettes Jail, and then they were sent to Compiegne Camp, under German occupation. Responding to another communiqué sent by the Turkish Consul-General the Marseilles Area Police Chief replied that he would deal with the matter and keep the Consul informed. Behic was furious. Clear and concise instructions were wired to the Marseilles Consulate-General on January 27, stating what needed to be done in case such situations were repeated..

"Our Jewish citizens whose documents are in order must not be exposed to this compulsory labor force. In case such an adverse situation does arise, then we must ensure that those citizens are provided protection. Local police chiefs, who are to be reminded of these and other similar instructions, will have to intervene with the pertinent authorities whenever deemed necessary."

The Consul-General and his staff had to remain insistent and intervene immediately with all revelant authorities, whether they were French or German, whenever such incidents occurred.

LIFE & DEATH DIPLOMACY

* * *

Behic wasn't the only person in the legation who put his career and his life on the line to save Turkish Jews. In 1994 Necdet Kent related his experiences as a Vice- Consul. One evening, the doorbell rang at his Marseilles home. Opening the door, Kent found himself face-to-face with Sadi İşcan, a young Jewish man who worked at the Consulate as a translator. After catching his breath, İşcan told Kent that some Jews had been rounded up in another part of town, the same way they had been captured in the Old Harbor district a few weeks before. There were quite a number of Turkish citizens among those arrested. İşcan said that they had been taken to the Saint Charles train station.

There was no time to lose. Kent quickly put on his shoes and he and İşcan went to the station arriving just as the train was about to leave. Starting at the front cattle car, the two men yelled out in Turkish: "Are any Turks in this car?" Hearing nothing they hurried down the platform yelling the same thing the door of each cattle car. From the last two cars they heard voices shouting "We're Turkish! We're Turkish!"

Running to those cars Kent shouted that he was the Turkish Vice –Consul. Suddenly he was taken aback. He was hit with the overwhelming stench of stock animals and the sign on the outside of one of the cars: *Railcar capacity 20 head of cattle and half a ton of hay.*

The commotion these two men caused did not go unnoticed by the German officer on duty.

He ran to the cars demanding that Kent and İşcan stop what they were doing immediately. Defiant but still level headed, Kent mustered all the diplomatic 'cool' he could and demanded that his Turkish citizens be released from the car. Seemingly unimpressed, the officer looked at the diplomatic I.D. commenting that there were only Jews in the car.

"You're making a big mistake. I'm a Turkish diplomat and I'm requesting you to correct this mistake by having these people disembark from the train."

"I'm assigned to this station and my orders are to load up the Jews who have been brought to the station and send them on their way."

Just as the German officer made a move to lock the sliding door of the train car, Kent pushed the door open, grabbed İşcan and jumped inside. The wretched people in the railroad car watched this spectacle with total bewilderment. The officer was yelling at Kent to get out and Kent braced himself in the doorway refusing to leave. These were his people and he wasn't going to leave them. The German clamped the lock down on their door, went to the last wagon locking that door, too, then blew his whistle for the train to leave. As the train began to move, Necdet Kent and Sadi İşcan looked at each other in total shock. They were now sharing the same fate as their Turkish Jews.

Kent may have been at the beginning of his diplomatic career, but he understood how crucial this matter was. He had held several meetings with the authorities and had carried out the orders of his ambassador, which authorized intervention, to the point where Kent was now traveling on one of those infamous "Destination Unknown" trains! Shortly after the German returned to his station office, his door flew open and two men rushed inside asking if he had seen two young men come through. The officer told them that not only did they come but they left on that last train.   Sadi İşcan's father couldn't believe his ears and Bedi'i Arbel wanted to know what train, where is the train headed and why the two young men were even on the train.

"They refused to come down, saying they had orders. I couldn't get them to jump down; they ended up leaving the station with the train!"

Bedi'i Arbel and Sadi İşcan's father rushed to Arbel's home to call the Ambassador. Arbel explained to Iscan's father that the Gestapo Headquarters in Vichy was located right next door to the Turkish Embassy and that he was sure the Ambassador would save them.

Telephoning the Ambassador, Bedi'i Arbel gave him the details.

"Okay, I will take care of it. Seems young Necdet went a bit beyond the call of duty, but bravo. He did the right thing. He had no other choice. Now don't worry about a thing, I'll do everything in my power to save those young men and our Turkish citizens too."

The duty officer at Gestapo Headquarters knew the Turkish ambassador, but he had never seen him storm into Gestapo headquarters as if he were attacking it! With Zeki at his side, my grandfather demanded to see von Nidda and began yelling at the duty officer and waving his cane at him The duty officer wanted to know what was the matter but Behic kept yelling to see von Nidda then added "Two countries are headed for a major crisis and you're wasting time asking me questions?"

The duty officer liked the old guy but he knew von Nidda would want to know why the Turkish Ambassador demanded to see him.

"Believe me, if you don't call Krug von Nidda over here right now, you'll be making a huge mistake, one that I'm sure he'll make you pay for!" shouted the ambassador.

Feeling helpless, the duty officer went over to his desk, jotted down a short note and shoved it into an envelope.

"Why don't you just call him?" asked the ambassador.

"Herr Krug von Nidda is attending a reception this evening. But let me assure you, Mr. Ambassador, I'm going to send a car with this note. I'm sure he'll soon be here."

The duty officer knew that even though von Nidda became angry with the Turkish ambassador because he was obsessed with aiding Jews, he also had a great deal of respect for the ambassador, so he was fairly certain that von Nidda wouldn't get upset when he received a note from the Gestapo Duty Officer that the Turkish Ambassador was refusing to leave Gestapo headquarters until he saw the German-Consul about a very urgent matter. The Ambassador even refused to take a seat, preferring to stand although he had to support himself on his cane.

Before long, von Nidda arrived and with a bit humorously quipped: "For goodness sake, Your Excellency, what could be so urgent and crucial? I was dying of curiosity on the way here. Did Turkey finally join the war?"

The German-Consul immediately saw that the Turkish ambassador did not have his customary smile on his face.

"Because of you, we're one step away from joining the war," fumed the ambassador.

"One of your train station commanders locked up two freight cars of my citizens and as if that wasn't enough, he threw in two of my Consulate-General staff. God only knows where they are now." Behiç paused to steady himself on his cane. "Not only that, but one of those men was not any ordinary Consulate-General staff member, but a diplomat; the Vice-Consul himself. We've got a diplomatic scandal here, and that's putting it mildly! What was this station commander of yours thinking? Do you want to throw away the relationship that we've built up over the past three years? Let me put it to you another way, while the relations of two old friends and allied nations are currently where everyone wants them to be, do you want to irreparably destroy them?"

Von Nidda wanted to take the discussion out of the hall and into his office but my grandfather dug in his heels.

"As long as my citizens and my diplomats remain on that train, wild horses couldn't drag me from this spot. If you don't intervene in this big mess, then a crisis between our two countries will be unavoidable and when I explain everything that has happened here down to the very last detail to my President, I'm sure he's going to immediately re-evaluate relations between Berlin and Turkey. If you can't obtain a satisfactory result right now, then I'll be leaving immediately to inform my President without wasting another minute."

Quickly Von Nidda asked Behic to wait for a few minutes and then rushed straight into his office. This was going to be a difficult decision to make, because the train was already eastbound. To make matters worse, he was under an immense amount of pressure regarding the Jewish Question.

The situation on the train was dire. People were packed into filthy cattle cars and the stench was overwhelming. Children were crying. Mothers were moaning. Fathers were asking what was going to happen to their families. Necdet Kent tried to remain calm, but the minutes and then the hours passed as the train continued it's journey eastward into the cold darkness.

Sadi İşcan feared for his life. Despite being a Turkish citizen he, too, was Jewish just like all these passengers. Being Turkish wasn't going to save him at their final destination. Sensing this, Kent told him to remain calm; he was under the protection of the Turkish Consul General.

"But I'm also Jewish!"

"Nothing's going to happen; you're a diplomatic Jew."

"That may be, but there's nothing diplomatic about this train."

My grandfather never moved from his spot at Gestapo headquarters. He knew something was going on but he waited for von Nidda.

Von Nidda came out of his office announcing that all the contacts had been made and now all that was left to do was wait. But my grandfather never budged. Finally the pain in his right knee forced him to sit down and von Nidda sat down next to him on the wooden bench in front of the Duty Officer's room. Because it was cold, he suggested that Behic go back to the embassy and wait there assuring him that von Nidda himself would keep him informed. My grandfather looked at him, shook his head no, and remained where he was. He had no intention of speaking until this incident was brought to a satisfactory conclusion. His silence forced Krug von Nidda into a state of silence which seemed to engulf the entire German Gestapo headquarters..

There was finally silence in the railroad cars where the Turkish Jews seemed to accept their fate. Children were now asleep; mothers, too. Only the fathers stood silently staring out into the darkness while the two helpless diplomats remained with their hopeless citizens in a cattle car whose original stench was now mixed with the smell of vomit.

Sitting on the wooden bench next to the silent German-Consul, Behiç remembered when he sat next to German Generals 25 years ago in Turkey. It seemed nothing had changed for him. His fate, his destiny seemed to evolve around these people. What had he done to deserve this? He had avoided picking Berlin when the post was offered by his President, choosing Paris, thinking it was the city of lights and cafes. But because of the Germans, he was only there a few months. Now he was in a city run by Germans, sitting next to another German General.

Behiç wrote that ever since the Turkish Embassy had been established in France, no other ambassador had put up with what he did. No one has ever faced such problems and difficulties. For a 67 year old cripple it was starting to be a bit much. He wrote that "Everyone had tons of fun in Paris and France. I, on the other hand, suffered immeasurably."

A telephone ringing from inside the duty officer's room broke the silence and Behiç's thoughts. No one moved. They waited for the duty officer to give von Nidda a note. Behiç held his breath.

"Mr. Ambassador, my contacts have produced a result. The train will be stopped. Your Consulate-General staff member and Vice-Consul will be taken off the train."

"Fine," said Behiç in a harsh voice. "But what about my Turkish citizens?"

"All those who are Turkish will be taken off the train as well; the others will stay on board!"

"They are all Turkish citizens."

"How do you know?"

"That's what my Marseilles Consul told me."

God forgive me, Behiç thought to himself. But if a lie could save all the Jews on that train, Turkish and non-Turkish, then Behiç was prepared to lie. He hoped God would understand.

Krug von Nidda summoned the duty wireless officer. "Get this telegraph off to all stations north of Marseilles!" The German-Consul then turned to Behiç. "As the matter has been taken care of, allow me to see you to the gate, Mr. Ambassador."

Behiç refused to get up. "I have no intention of leaving until I see a wire that everyone has been taken off the train."

Several hours after leaving Marseilles, the Jewish transport train slowly pulled into Arles station and stopped. Children woke up and started to cry waking everyone who had been able to fall asleep. A platoon of German soldiers marched double-time towards the last cars. A German voice shouting orders grated on everyone's ears. Kent rose to his feet and stood in front of the closed door. He wasn't sure what he was going to say if and when the door opened and prayed he would find the right words, say the right thing that might save them all. The heavy door slid open and below on the platform was a high ranking SS officer, obviously not the station commander.

"Are you the Turkish diplomat on this train?" asked the German officer.

"We both are," he said, pulling Sadi İşcan up next to him.

"Would you two please come down from there?"

"No, we won't," said Kent, surprised at his own directness. "We boarded this train to protect the rights of the all the Turkish citizens on this train. If they aren't allowed off as well, I have not carried out my duty."

The German officer peaked inside the door to his left and then to his right. His face went sour as the putrid stench overpowered his nasal passages. Once more he glanced to the left and right side of the Turkish diplomats. Then he asked: "Which ones are your citizens?"

Silence. Even the young children were quiet. Everyone at once seemed to hold their breaths.

Someone was about to decide their fate. Most of them were not Turkish.

Kent glanced around as if he were counting heads then said, "They're all Turkish citizens. That's why I boarded the train back in Marseilles."

The German officer stared into Necdet Kent's eyes for a few seconds and Kent stared right back.

"Have all the Turks get off the train."

"They're all Turkish."

"Then get them all off, right now!" shouted the German commander.

Kent turned to the huddle mass of exhausted Jews and shouted out in Turkish: "Hurry up, what are you waiting for? Get out of here and bring all the other Jews with you. Tell them not to say a word, just to pretend they are Turkish."

The German soldiers stood attention, their rifles across their chests, as one cattle car disgorged its passengers. While Sadi □şcan helped everyone down from the first cattle car, Kent rushed back to the second car and gave the same instructions in Turkish. Within a few minutes both wagons were empty.

As soon as the German commander saw that all the passengers were on the platform he signaled to a conductor who blew his whistle and the train immediately began to move. No one wanted to be responsible for a transport being one minute late even if it no longer had all the Jews onboard.

Without checking anyone's papers, the German officer left with his soldiers.

The instant the Germans disappeared from sight, more than 80 Jews surrounded Necdet Kent, trying to touch and kiss his hand. But Kent did not have time for congratulations. Breaking away from the crowd, he shouted: "Sadi, we've got to find some trucks to transport these people back to Marseilles!"

After reading the telegram in his hands several times, Behiç Erkin finally stood up and spoke German for the first time in his life. "Danke schön, Herr Krug!"

"May I say something, My Esteemed Mr. Ambassador?".

"Of course."

"Now I understand why the German commanders serving in the Ottoman Army during World War I, both loathed you and held you in the greatest esteem. You deserved Germany's highest medal."

Lt. General Krug von Nidda saluted the ambassador, then abruptly turned and strode back into Gestapo headquarters.

As he slowly walked back to the Turkish Embassy, an amusing smile crept across Behiç's face and for a few seconds he forgot he was only standing thanks to his cane.

THE AMBASSADOR RECALLED

* * *

To say that Grandfather's intervention did not go down well in Berlin would be a gross understatement. It never happened before and would never happen again. From that day on, the German Foreign Ministry put pressure on their ambassador in Ankara to convince the Turkish government that it would be in the best interests of both countries if the "trouble-maker" were recalled. Although Behiç was aware that the Germans were upset with him, he did not realize that many Turkish newspapers that were actually pro-German, nor that there were many politicians in the Turkish government who thought his actions might jeopardize Turkey's neutrality in the war. Perhaps another ambassador would have kept his head down for a while to let the pressure to recall him subside. Behiç could not do that. After all he was a general and generals usually pursue a retreating enemy.

Behiç also forced Berlin and the Vichy government to push back the final deadline for the evacuation of Jewish Turks from France from January 31, 1943 to March 31, 1943. During that time, the Turkish Embassy organized several more train convoys of predominantly Jewish Turkish citizens to Istanbul. While the Nazis were transporting hundreds of thousands to the extermination camps, the father of the Turkish railways was sending thousands of Turkish Jews by rail in another direction.

Although the Turkish President had personally given his ambassador in France permission to carry out these unusual duties, the intense pressure Berlin applied on Ankara forced them to recall Behiç in August of 1943. Naturally, Behiç protested. When his first term as ambassador had officially ended he convinced the Turkish President and the Turkish Foreign Ministry to extend his tour of duty for another year. But in the end, the only concession he could pry out of the Turkish government was for them to place the blame of his recall on the Germans. In the Washington Post, the headline read: Turkey recalls Envoy to Vichy; Ties Strained. The subhead line read: Strong Nazi Curbs on Ambassador's Activities Blamed.

Behiç's 40-year old daughter Reside met him in Paris to accompany him home. Also with him on his return journey was his beautiful blonde 29-year-old French secretary, Georgette, who for the next five years would be Behiç's "governess," as he called her in his memoirs. He may have been in his late sixties and needed a cane, but obviously he wasn't *that* old! Traveling with him until Budapest was Bodo Stomadis, Behiç's faithful and loyal butler for 23 years. Bodo, his wife and their child were going to Hungary to visit his father-in-law. Later Bodo returned to Paris and worked at the embassy until 1958 earning the praise of every Turkish ambassador who succeeded Behiç. Despite his recall, the transportation of Turkish Jews to Istanbul did not completely stop. Using the guidelines Behiç established, the next Turkish ambassador tried to carry on where Behiç left off.

What my grandfather was able to do was nothing short of miraculous. Behiç had directed his staff to provide Turkish citizenship vouchers for around 10,000 Jews. He also personally succeeded in obtaining official approval from France and Germany for these Turkish Jews to be evacuated and sent to Turkey during the war. He and his staff arranged journeys that saved the lives of around 18,800 Jews. Even though he wasn't there to see the final freedom train leave France, he had instructed his remaining staff exactly on what needed to be done.

Behiç and his staff and Ankara insisted that they were saving Turkish Jews because they were Turkish citizens, not because they were Jews. But the fact remains that of all the Turkish citizens living in France, only the Jews were at risk. Throughout his life my grandfather helped a people in need whether it was the Turkish railroad workers 20 years earlier, or the Turkish Jews in France during the Holocaust. His conscience rejected any injustice he came across.

In his memoir, Behiç wrote: "The treatment of children, women, men, mothers and fathers as though they were mere herds of animals, separating members of the same family from each other and shipping them to indeterminate destinations..."

Behiç seldom wrote the word "Jew" in his memoirs. He just called them "people in need...Turkish citizens in need." It was this sentence, which was written in a communiqué he sent to Ankara, that best reflects the voice of Behiç's conscience.

In June 2003 Yad Vashem <u>The Holocaust Martyrs' and Heroes' Remembrance Authority</u> awarded its highest honor, the *Righteous Among Nations* to Brazilian diplomat Luis Martins de Souza-Dantas for helping Jews in France escape the Holocaust. It was estimated he saved 800 people; 425 Jews, and the rest being people considered undesirables according to Nazism.

Neither Turkish Ambassador Behiç Erkin nor any member of his staff was ever so honored by the State of Israel. But since 1945 every time a new Turkish ambassador presents his credentials to the President of Argentina, a delegation of former French Jews, now citizens of Argentina, meet with the new Turkish ambassador to thank his country once again for what Ambassador Behiç Erkin and his staff did to save their lives.

BEHİÇ ERKİN

In 1918, Erkin was honored with the Iron Cross Medal first degree,
the highest rank medal of German State.

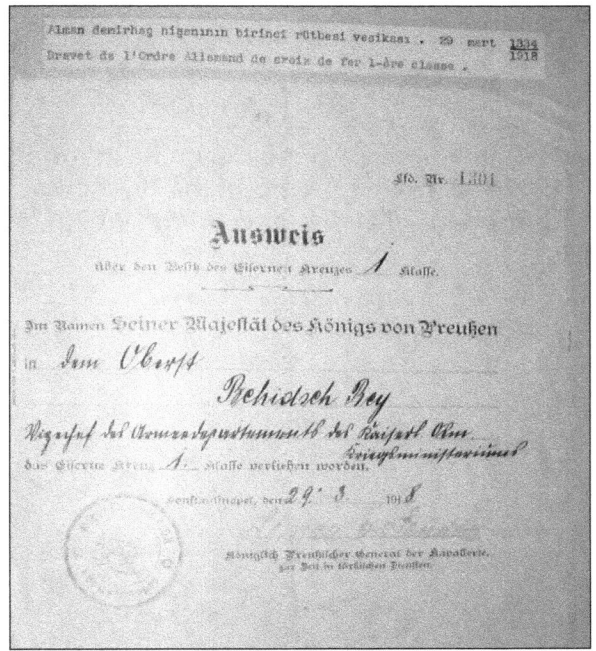

Certificate for the German Iron Cross Medal first degree.

French newspapers anouncing the new Turkish Ambassador on
September 3, 1939 Visiting the "Tomb of the Unknown Soldier", Arc
de Triomphe de l'Étoile, on September 2, 1938.

On the left is Prime Minister Pierre Laval; in the middle is Ambassador Behiç Erkin; and on the right is President Philippe Petain.

The Jews waiting in front of the Turkish Consulate General in Paris, in 1943 to get Turkish Passports and visas to enable them to go to Turkey.

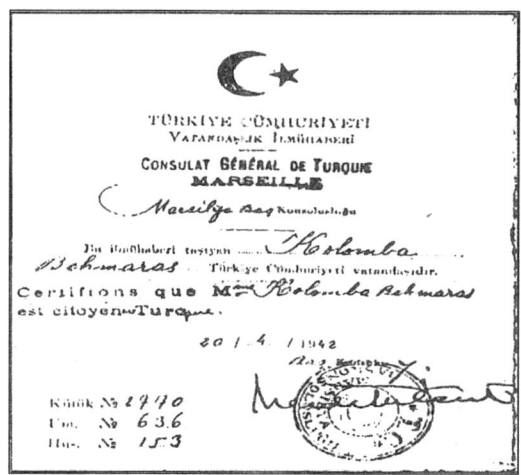

When the Germans occupied France, the only thing that determined whether thousands of people would live or die was a piece of paper stamped with a CRESCENT and STAR.

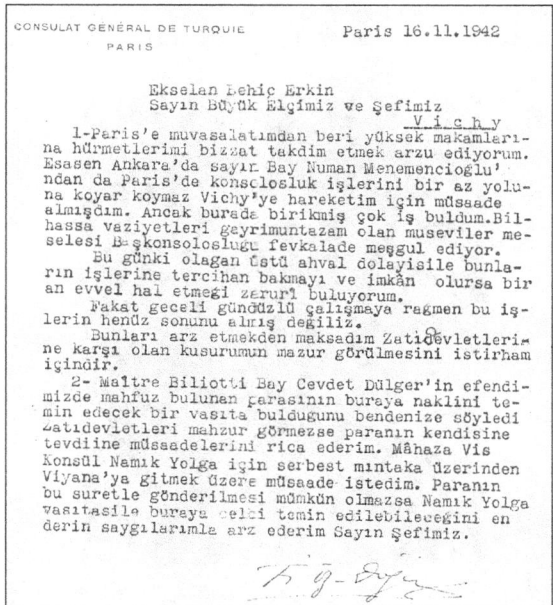

The original communication between the Consul General Şefik Özdosğancı and the Ambassador Behiç Erkin. On the 3rd paragraph it is written that Turkish diplomats are working day and night to issue Turkish documents to the Jews. See page 139 for whole translation of the document.

175

The telegram of Dr.Samuel Abravaya thanking Ambassador Behiç Erkin for rescuing his daughter and sun-in-law from deportation to death camps.

The original telegram is archived in the İnkilap Tarihi Müzesi (Revolution History Museum), Ankara University, since 1958.

M. Léon BLUM

He was the first Jewish Prime Minister in French history elected in 1936. Between 1936-1947 he was elected three times to that the office.

Eski Fransa Baş Vekili Leon Blumun Hapishaneden yazdığı Mektub.

Bourassol, 22 Février.

Monsieur l'Ambassadeur,

Je vous prie d'accepter mon plus cordial remerciement pour le soin que vous avez pris de me faire communiquer la bonne nouvelle par Monsieur le Président Cavro. Mais je vous prie aussi — permettez-moi de vous prie que je vous prie surtout — le transmettre au Président Ismet Inönü l'expression de ma profonde gratitude. Je lui dois le plus sensible soulagement qui pût être apporté aux conditions de ma vie personnelle. Et ce qui ajouté encore à ma satisfaction, c'est que son intervention amicale n'a pas bénéficié seulement à mon fils, mais à tous les camarades de camp dont il partage désormais le sort.

Veuillez agréer, je vous prie, Monsieur l'Ambassadeur, l'assurance de ma déférente et sympathique considération,

Léon Blum

The original letter written by the former French Prime Minister Leon Blum, thanking Ambassador Behiç Erkin for the help, he and the President Inonu has done for his sun whom captured by the Nazi's.

The original of this letter is archived in the İnkilap Tarihi Müzesi (Revolution History Museum), Ankara University, file 12 of the "Personal Red Files of Behiç Erkin", since 1958.

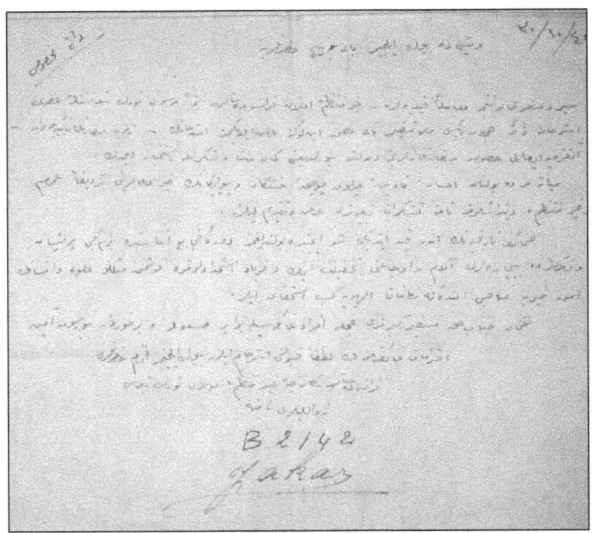

The letter of gratitude written to Behic Erkin in the name of thousands of Turkish origin French Jews who faced certain death during the Holocaust.

THE SECIAL NOTE OF THE AUTHOR EMIR KIVIRCIK:
"The letter of gratitude written to Behic Erkin in the name of thousands of French Jews who faced certain death during the Holocaust means more to our family than any medal ever could."

For your eyes only   *10.30.1942*
To His Excellency Behiç Erkin, Our Vichy Ambassador;
We are grateful to you for allowing us to send the petition we wrote to President İsmet İnönü in order to explain the matter regarding the Turkish-Jewish population who are of Turkish descent but who have not maintained their registration on a regular basis in compliance with the deportation law which is enforced in France. We learned with great satisfaction of the role undertaken by your Embassy

and the great efforts exerted regarding the assistance afforded to the Jews.

All the senior citizens, women, children, the disabled, and poor citizens in our patronage offer you a prayer of good fortune on behalf of all our fellow non-registered Jews with all our hearts.

The exalted heart and soul of Behiç, who has lessened the burden of households, who has lessened the pain of the miserable and wretched survivors like us and who has acknowledged our appeal for assistance during this unmitigated disaster which we find ourselves in today, one that is rarely found in the pages of history. He who conducts beneficent work, of course, garners accolades and deserves such accolades.

May God Bless Our Ambassador along with all the members of his family and keep them in good health and spirits, Amen.

Our Exalted Ambassador, please accept our highest respects.

On behalf of the thousands of poor, irregular Jewish Turks living in France.

B 2142
Yakar

The original copy of this letter is preserved in the İnkilap Tarihi Müzesi (Revolution History Museum), on the premises of the Turkish Revolution Institution at Ankara University. It is registered in Catalogue Tite-A6, Row No.113, Box No.190 with the entry, "Letter written on behalf of our Jewish citizens in France."

Turkey Recalls Envoy to Vichy; Ties Strained

Strong Nazi Curbs On Ambassador's Activities Blamed

By Frank Brutto
Associated Press Staff Writer

Bern, Switzerland, June 17.— Turkey has recalled Behic Erkin, its Ambassador to France, in protest against strong German restrictions on his embassy in Vichy, a Turkish diplomatic source said today.

Washington Post June 17, 1943
"STRONG NAZI CURBS ON AMBASSADOR'S ACTIVITIES BLAMED"

Ceremony awarding the Grand-Croix Medal, the highest degree
of Legion d'Honneur, on 23 July 1943. On the left is Marshall Petain
and on the right is Behiç Erkin.

Behiç Bey artık anıt mezarında

Kurtuluş Savaşı'nın en önemli komutanlarından biri olan Behiç Erkin, yıllardır Enveriye'de bakımsız bir mezarda tren seslerini dinliyordu. En sonunda bu büyük komutana yakışır bir anıt mezar yapıldı.

Enveriye İstasyonu'nda yıllardır bakımsız bir mezar duruyordu. Hatta Eskişehir'de bu mezar ile ilgili çeşitli rivayetler de çıkmıştı. Hikayeye göre, aşkına karşılık bulamayan bir genç kendini burada trenin altına atmıştı. Halbuki o mezar, Atatürk'ün en yakın arkadaşı, Çanakkale Harbi'nin, Kurtuluş Savaşı'nın en kritik komutanlarından, demiryollarını işleten ilk Türk olan, Milli İstihbarat Teşkilatına, Emekli Sandığını kuran ve Türkiye için daha birçok yeniliğe imza atan Behiç Erkin'e ait.
Hemen yanı başımızda yatan ancak tanımadığımız Behiç Bey'i, bugün hala büyük bir saygı ve minnetle anan insanlar var, üstelik Fransa'da. İkinci Dünya Savaşı sırasında Fransa'daki büyükelçimiz Behiç Bey'i hayatları boyunca unutmayan binlerce insan...

18 bin 200 kişiyi Nazilerin elinden kurtardı

O dönemde Nazi yönetiminin kuklası durumunda olan Fransa hükümeti ülkesinde yaşayan Yahudilerin listesini Nazilere verirken, Behiç Erkin kurtarabildiği kadar insan hayatı kurtarmak için canını dışine taktı ve Fransa'daki Musevilere Türkiye Cumhuriyeti vatandaşlık belgesi verdi. Sahip olduğu 1. dereceden Demir Haç madalyasının gücünü kullanarak Nazilere. "Türkiye savaşta tarafsız bir ülkedir. Tarafsız bir ülkenin vatandaşlarına dokunamazsınız" diyerek Fransa'da yaşayan Türk Yahudilerini Nazi takibinden kurtardı. Ayrıca koruma isteyen tüm Fransız vatandaşlarına Türkiye Cumhuriyeti vatandaşlığına geçme yolunu açtı. Türkiye'den trenler getirterek ya da trenlere ay yıldız astırarak, Nazi egemenliği altındaki bütün Avrupa'dan bu trenleri geçirerek Türkiye'ye getirdi ve

anlatılınca çok etkilendim. O kadar çok şeye imza atmış ki... Dolayısıyla hemen anneme gittim ama ikna etmek zor oldu. Annem hala bozuktu gönlü. Ama artık daha bilinçliydim, yaş kemale ermişti. İki gün boyunca bana Behiç Bey'i anlattı. Neden bunları bilmiyoruz diye sordum. O zaman annem dedi ki, "Babanız siz çok küçükken vefat etti. Ben iki tane erkek evlat büyütmek için hayatla savaştım...

Behiç Bey Eskişehirli değil, neden mezarı için burayı vasiyet etmiş?

Atatürk dedeme, "Ben cephelerde ne yapılması gerektiğini biliyorum ama cephelere nasıl asker getirileceğini bilmiyorum. Bunu başaracak tek kişi sensin. Sen askerleri getir, ben cephelerde başarıyı gerçekleştireyim" demiş. Dedem

Emir Kıvırcık visiting grandpa Behiç Erkin in his mausoleum in the city of Eskişehir.

Lazare Rousso with Emir Kıvırcık in Hürriyet newspaper on
February 18, 2007

"How did Emir Kıvırcık meet Lazare Rousso who had been rescued
by Kivircik's grandfather?"

What is written in Hebrew on the tombstone:
Left : David, died in battle in Jerusalem, 17 years old
Right: Josef (Papiko) Born in Turkey, Died in battle in Neveh Yaakov,
20 years old.
In the middle: Sons of Sharlot and Abraham, Their mother is crying
for them, refuses to find console. Their death saved their Nation.
Director of the Righteous Among the Nations Section of **Yad Vashem**
Museum, Israel Mrs. Irina Steinfeld has informed the" Union of Jews
from Turkey" in Israel the followings:
Mother name Charlotte, father name Avraam,
Family left for Hamburg from Istanbul in 1930,
Big brother name YOSEF born in Istanbul 22.06.1927,
Young brother DAVID is born in Hamburg in 07.09.1930,
Family left for France in 1931,
Family returned to Turkey in 1943.
According to Irina Steinfeld this is the period Behic Erkin was in charge.
Family left Turkey and went to Israel at the same year, 1943.
This two brothers has lost their lives during the war for establishing Israel in 1948.
DAVID died in 12.06.1948
YOSEF died in 28.03.1948

Ambassador Behiç Erkin personally told Aron Angel that he would send Angel to Turkey and he did. On page 4 of a brochure prepared by The Quincentennial Foundation (500. Yil Vakfı) for a special event recognizing Angle in November 2008, he expressed his gratitude for Behiç Erkin:
"Our Ambassador Behiç Erkin took his place in the history as the symbol of humanity."

Fransalı Yahudilerden Sarkozy'ye 'Türklere vefa borcu' hatırlatması

Ali İhsan Aydın | Paris

Zaman, Paris, September 26, 2008.

September 24, 2008, Holocaust survivors who were sent out of Nazi occupied France to Turkey gathered in Paris to recount their stories and thank the Turkish diplomats and the Republic of Turkey for providing a safe haven during World war II. The six survivors are Albert Carel, Arnette Bules, Claire Romi, Rose Illel-Hatem, Rafael Illel and Albert Çiprut.

THE PRESIDENT

Jerusalem, April 2, 2008

Mr. Emir Kivircik

Dear Mr. Kivircik,

It was a distinct pleasure meeting you when I was in Turkey last, and I want to thank you most sincerely for remembering to send me your interesting book.

I wholly agree with you that Jews and Muslims should be able once again to live together in peace, and work together to build a better future for the next generations. I believe that education is the key to better understanding, tolerance and a constructive dialogue among our two religions. I therefore urge all parties to invest today in tomorrow's leaders, in order to create harmony in the region and motivate the next generation to cooperate with one another for the benefit of all.

I appreciate your wise words and hope they will be heard by many.

Sincerely yours,

Shimon Peres

The letter of His Excellency Shimon Peres, The President of Israel to Emir Kıvırcık.

www.ingramcontent.com/pod-product-compliance
Lightning Source LLC
Chambersburg PA
CBHW062148280526
45788CB00001B/346